500 Recipes

Italian

Published in 2013
by Igloo Books Ltd
Cottage Farm
Sywell
Northants
NN6 0BJ
www.igloobooks.com

Food photography and recipe development: PhotoCuisine UK
Front and back cover images © PhotoCuisine UK

SHE001 0913
2 4 6 8 10 9 7 5 3 1
ISBN: 978-1-78197-901-3

Printed and manufactured in China

500 Recipes
Italian

igloobooks

CONTENTS

STARTERS AND SIDES

1

SERVES 4

Fresh Fruit Minestrone

PREPARATION TIME:
15 MINUTE + MACERATING TIME

COOKING TIME: 15 MINUTES

INGREDIENTS

FOR THE SOUP BASE:
400 ml / 14 fl. oz / 1 ⅗ cups water
80 g / 3 oz / ⅓ cup caster (superfine)
sugar
1 vanilla pod
sprig of mint
strip of lemon zest

2 apricots, stoned and chopped
2 peaches, stoned and chopped
200 g / 7 oz / 2 ⅔ cups strawberries,
hulled and halved
100 g / 4 oz / 1 cup raspberries
2 kiwi fruit, peeled and chopped
pistachio ice cream, to serve

- Heat the water in a pan with the sugar.
- Split the vanilla pod in half down the middle, scrape out the seeds and place both the seeds and pod in the pan.
- Add the mint and zest and simmer without stirring until the sugar has dissolved, then remove from the heat and leave to cool.
- Stir the fruits into the syrup and leave to macerate for 30 minutes or so. You may want to add a little lemon juice.
- Serve with the ice cream.

Melon Minestrone

2

Instead of kiwi fruit, add half a peeled, seeded and chopped melon.

3

MAKES 6-8

Olive and Asiago Pizzas

PREPARATION TIME:
45 MINUTES + PROVING TIME

COOKING TIME: 8-10 MINUTES

INGREDIENTS

FOR THE PIZZA DOUGH:
400 g / 14 oz / 2 ⅔ cups strong white
bread flour
100 g / 3 ½ oz / ⅔ cup finely ground
semolina flour
½ tbsp salt
1 x 7 g sachet dried yeast
½ tbsp caster (superfine) sugar
350 ml /12 fl. oz / 1 ⅖ cup lukewarm
water

FOR THE TOPPING:
1 onion, sliced
2 tbsp butter
4 handfuls black olives, halved or
left whole
75 g / 3 oz / ⅔ cup Asiago cheese per
pizza
thyme

- Pour the flour and salt into a bowl and make a well.
- Add the yeast and sugar to the water, mix and leave for a few minutes. When frothing, pour into the well.
- Slowly bring in the flour from around the insides and mix into the water.
- When it starts coming together, use your hands and pat it into a ball. Knead the dough for 10 minutes.
- Flour and cover with film and leave to rest for 30 minutes. Meanwhile, cook the onion in the butter in a pan until deep golden in colour and caramelised.
- Preheat the oven to 240°C (220° fan) / 475F / gas 9. Flour the surface, tear off a piece of dough and roll into a rough circle about 0.5cm thick.
- Dust each one with a little flour and lay out on the surface. Top each one with olives, onions and sliced cheese. Place on a preheated baking sheet for 8-10 minutes until golden.

Garlic and Parmesan Pizzas

4

Try topping with a head of peeled garlic crushed to a paste with salt and olive oil, then sprinkling with a little Parmesan for garlic bread.

5

MAKES 2

Courgette Focaccia

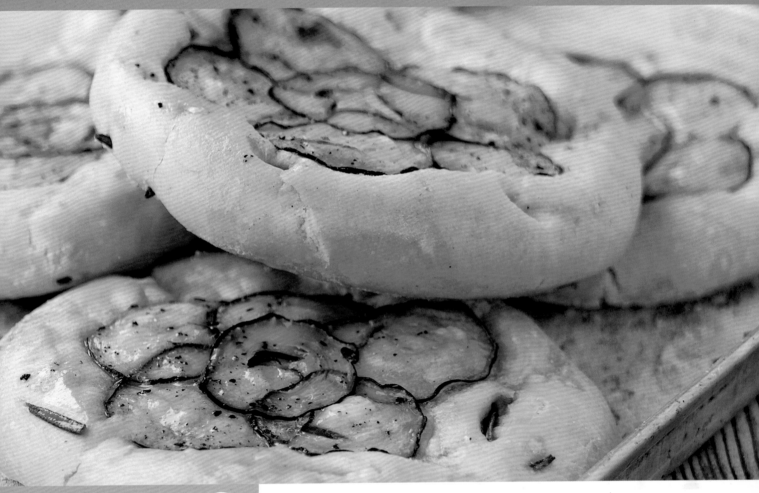

Courgette and Mozzarella Focaccia

6

Add cubes of mozzarella over the courgette for a melting top.

Courgette and Parmesan Focaccia

7

Sprinkle grated Parmesan over the courgette.

Aubergine and Mozzarella Focaccia

8

Replace the courgette with slices of aubergine (eggplant) and add cubes of mozzarella on top.

PREPARATION TIME: 40 MINUTES
+ 2 HOURS PROVING TIME

COOKING TIME: 20 MINUTES

....

INGREDIENTS

750 g / 1 ¼ lb / 3 cups '00' flour
½ tsp salt
2 tsp fast-action dried yeast
150 ml / 5 fl. oz / ⅔ cup extra virgin olive oil
450 ml / 16 fl. oz / 1 ⅘ cups lukewarm water
2 courgettes (zucchinis, very thinly sliced
coarse sea salt
rosemary leaves

- Sift the flour and salt into a bowl and make a well in the centre.
- Pour 50 ml of the oil into the flour, add the yeast and rub together with your fingers. Pour in 400 ml of the water and mix until the dough comes together.
- Tip the dough onto a floured surface and knead for 10 minutes until smooth. Place in a lightly oiled bowl, cover with film and leave to rise in a warm place.
- After 1 hour, take the dough out of the bowl, punch out the air and divide in to two balls.
- Roll into 2 circles and place in 2 oiled pizza pans. Cover with film and leave to rise for 30 minutes. Preheat the oven to 200° C (180° fan) / 400F / gas 6.
- Uncover push your fingertips in to make deep dimples. Layer the top with the courgette slices.
- Drizzle with oil and top with sprigs of rosemary and salt. Bake for 20 minutes until risen.
- Drizzle with the remaining oil and cool on a wire rack before serving.

9

MAKES 3

Ciabatta Bread

PREPARATION TIME: 30 MINUTES

COOKING TIME: 25 MINUTES

INGREDIENTS

500 g / 1 lb 12 oz / 3 ⅓ cups '00' flour
380 ml / 13 fl. oz / 1 ¾ cups water
25 g / 1 oz / 2 tbsp fresh yeast
1 tbsp olive oil
1 tbsp salt

- Mix half the flour with half the water in a large bowl and add half the yeast. Mix together well for a few minutes, then cover and leave to rise overnight.
- Next day add the remaining flour and yeast and mix well. Gradually add the water and oil, mixing it together in a food mixer for a few minutes.
- Then add the salt and mix until you have a very sticky dough.
- Transfer the dough to a large oiled bowl and leave to rise, covered, for one hour.
- Move from the bowl and leave to rest on a floured work surface for 30 minutes.
- Preheat the oven to 240°C (220° fan) / 475F / gas 9.
- Pull the dough into 3 long flat slipper shapes.
- Place on a baking sheet and leave to rest for 10 minutes.
- Bake in the oven for 25 minutes or until risen and golden brown. Transfer to a wire rack to cool.

Ciabatta with Mixed Herbs

10

Add dried mixed herbs into the mixture before kneading for an aromatic twist.

11

SERVES 4

Pan-fried Potatoes with Rosemary

PREPARATION TIME: 10 MINUTES

COOKING TIME: 35 MINUTES

INGREDIENTS

1kg / 2 lb 4 oz / 6 ⅔ cups waxy potatoes, diced
75 ml / 3 fl. oz / ⅓ cup olive oil, duck or goose fat
2 garlic cloves, lightly crushed
Rosemary sprigs
Sea salt

- Heat the fat in a large pan with the garlic.
- When the scent begins to rise add the potatoes and turn to coat in the hot fat. Add the rosemary.
- Turn the heat down to fairly low, cover the pan and cook for 15-20 minutes until the potatoes are golden on one side.
- Turn them over, cover again and cook for a further 10-15 minutes until tender and golden.
- Remove to kitchen paper, sprinkle with sea salt and serve.

Potatoes with Olives

12

Add a handful of mixed olives at the end of cooking.

MAKES 40

Ham and Mozzarella Crostini

- Preheat the oven to 180°C (160° fan) / 350F / gas 4. Slice the ficelle into rounds, about 1cm thick.
- Dab each one with a little oil and bake in the oven until lightly golden and crisp, for about 8 minutes.
- Spread each crostini with a little pesto, then top with the Parma ham.
- Slice the mozzarella thinly, then arrange it on top of the ham.
- Sprinkle over basil and capers before serving.

PREPARATION TIME: 30 MINUTES

COOKING TIME: 8 MINUTES

INGREDIENTS

1 ficelle
olive oil
1 small jar basil pesto
20 slices Parma ham
300 g / 10 ½ oz / 3 cups mozzarella cheese
small bunch basil leaves
2 tbsp capers, drained and chopped

Ham and Sun-dried Tomato Crostini

Swap the basil pesto for sun-dried tomato pesto.

SERVES 4

Breaded Risotto Balls

- Stir the tomato and Parmesan through the risotto.
- Shape into equal balls, pushing a small cube of mozzarella into the centre of each one and shaping the rice around it.
- Lay out the flour, egg and breadcrumbs on separate plates.
- Dip the risotto balls into the flour, then the egg, then the breadcrumbs.
- Heat the oil to 180°C / 400F or until a cube of bread sizzles when dropped in the oil. Fry the risotto balls until golden and crisp all over.
- Serve hot or warm.

PREPARATION TIME: 20 MINUTES

COOKING TIME: 10 MINUTES

INGREDIENTS

275g / 10 oz / 1 cup risotto (Arborio) rice, cooked
1 tbsp Parmesan, grated
1 tomato, seeded and finely diced
1 ball mozzarella, cut into small cubes
1 tbsp basil leaves
1 tbsp plain (all purpose) flour
1 egg, beaten
40g / 1 ½ oz / 1/3 cup breadcrumbs
vegetable oil, for deep frying

Breaded Risotto Balls with Courgette

Substitute the tomato for a courgette (zucchini) and cook in the same way.

17

MAKES 18

Italian Platter

PREPARATION TIME: 5 MINUTES

COOKING TIME: 8-12 MINUTES

INGREDIENTS

1 olive ciabatta
75 g / 3 oz / ⅔ cup farfalle
40 g / 1 ½ oz / ⅓ stick butter
4-6 slices Parma ham
rocket
FOR THE SALSA VERDE:
1 bunch flat leaf parsley
10 mint leaves
1 bunch basil leaves
4 anchovies
1 tbsp Dijon mustard
4 cornichons
1 tbsp capers
extra virgin olive oil
lemon juice
salt and pepper

- Cook the ciabatta according to packet instructions.
- Cook the pasta in boiling salted water according to packet instructions. Drain, toss in butter, season and keep warm.
- Place the ingredients for the sauce in a food processor and whiz, drizzling in the oil. Add the squeeze of a lemon.
- Arrange the ham into a bowl on a plate and fill with pasta.
- Slice the ciabatta and arrange alongside.
- Spoon the salsa into a ramekin and then spoon a little over the plate to decorate.

Creamy Italian Platter

18

Stir 2 tbsp crème fraiche into the salsa verde for a creamier, less punchy sauce.

19

SERVES 4

Chicken Breast Salad

PREPARATION TIME: 10 MINUTES

COOKING TIME: 8 MINUTES

INGREDIENTS

4 chicken breasts, skinned
2 tbsp olive oil
1 lemon, juiced
To serve
mixed salad leaves
2 celery stalks, finely chopped
Handful mixed olives, stoned and chopped

- Cut the chicken into large chunks.
- Heat oil in a pan and add the chicken. Cook until golden in patches and just cooked through. Season and remove to a plate.
- Squeeze the lemon juice into the pan off the heat and scrape furiously with a wooden spoon to deglaze – add a little water if necessary. Pour over the chicken.
- Meanwhile toss the salad and vegetables in a bowl. Add the hot chicken and pour over the cooking juices.
- Toss and serve.

Chicken Salad with Artichokes

20

Add sun-blushed tomatoes, halved, drained artichoke hearts or 1 tsp of drained capers for piquancy.

21

SERVES 6

Spicy Vermicelli

Spicy Leek Vermicelli

22

Use half a finely chopped leek instead of the spring onions and chives.

Nutmeg and Spinach Vermicelli

23

Substitute the spices for a little grated nutmeg and use 250g wilted baby spinach leaves instead of the onion and chives.

Spicy Vermicelli with Pepper

24

Sauté 1 diced sweet red pepper and 1 chopped chilli and cook the same.

PREPARATION TIME: 15 MINUTES

COOKING TIME:
4 MINUTES PER CAKE

....

INGREDIENTS

300 g / 10 ½ oz rice vermicelli nests
2 good pinches ground coriander
2 good pinches curry powder
2 spring onions (scallions), finely chopped
1 clove of garlic, finely chopped
1 bunch chives, finely chopped
30 g / 1 oz / ¼ stick butter
6 tbsp sunflower oil
salt and pepper

- Rehydrate the vermicelli noodles in boiling water and leave for about 6 minutes until tender.
- Drain and chop then place in a bowl.
- Add the coriander and curry powder, season well and then mix in the onions, garlic and chives.
- Heat the butter and ½ tbsp of oil in a blini pan and then spoon in a small amount of the noodle mixture.
- Cook for a few minutes on each side until golden and crisp.
- Remove to kitchen paper and drain and then keep warm in a low oven while cooking the remaining mixture.

25

SERVES 6

Deep-fried Ravioli

PREPARATION TIME:
45 MINUTES + RESTING TIME

COOKING TIME: 10 MINUTES

....

INGREDIENTS

FOR THE PASTA:
500 g / 1 lb 2 oz / 3 ⅓ cups Italian
'00' flour
6 eggs

FOR THE FILLING:
120 g / 4 oz / 1 cup Gruyere, grated
bunch of rocket, finely chopped
40 g / 1 ½ oz / ⅓ cup Parmesan,
grated
1 egg, beaten
bunch of flat leaf parsley, finely
chopped
salt and pepper
vegetable oil for deep frying

- Place the flour in a bowl and make a well in the centre. Crack the eggs into the well.
- Using a fork, beat the eggs and then draw in the flour a little at a time until the dough comes together. Knead the dough with your hands for 5 minutes.
- Cover with film and chill for 30 minutes. Mix together all of the filling ingredients and stir well.
- Using a pasta machine, roll out the dough into sheets 2 mm thick and 10 cm wide. Lay on a floured surface.
- Place 1 tsp of filling in the middle of the sheet at one end. Repeat all the way along at 5 cm intervals and then brush a little water around each filling in a circle.
- Place another sheet of pasta on top, then push the sheets together, around each mound of filling. Cut the ravioli into shapes using a knife or a crinkle-edged cutter.
- Blanch the ravioli in batches in a large saucepan of salted, boiling water for 1 minute before draining well.
- Heat the oil in a pan and cook the ravioli in batches until golden brown. Drain on kitchen paper and serve.

Deep-fried Spinach Ravioli

26

Substitute the rocket for finely chopped spinach for a milder flavour.

27

SERVES 4

Vegetarian Stuffed Peppers

PREPARATION TIME: 20 MINUTES

COOKING TIME: 15 MINUTES

....

INGREDIENTS

4 red peppers
2 tbsp olive oil

FOR THE FILLING
2 tbsp olive oil
1 courgette (zucchini), finely diced
2 tomatoes, finely diced
2 cloves garlic, finely chopped
4 tbsp breadcrumbs
1 tbsp oregano leaves
1 ball of Mozzarella, drained

- Preheat the oven to 200°C (180° fan) / 400F / gas 6.
- Cut the peppers in half and discard the seeds and white pith.
- Place in a roasting tin, drizzle with oil and season then bake for about 20 minutes until starting to soften. Set aside.
- Meanwhile heat the oil in a pan and fry the courgettes and garlic for 3 minutes, then add the tomatoes.
- Once the tomatoes have collapsed, stir in the breadcrumbs and oregano leaves and season.
- Remove from the heat, stir in the diced mozzarella and spoon into the cavities of the peppers.
- Return the stuffed peppers to the oven for 15 minutes or until bubbling.

Pancetta Stuffed Peppers

28

Add 2 packs cubed pancetta with the courgettes (zucchini) for a meat fix

29

MAKES 18

Ham, Olive and Rice Salad

- Cook the rice in boiling salted water for 13-14 minutes until just tender.
- Drain, stir with a fork and leave to cool.
- Meanwhile in a bowl, mix together the ham, olives, spring onions (scallions) and parsley, then tip in the rice.
- In another bowl whisk together the oil and vinegar and seasoning and taste – you may want to add more of something.
- Pour the dressing over the salad and mix well. Add more oil if necessary.

PREPARATION TIME: 10 MINUTES

COOKING TIME: 20 MINUTES

INGREDIENTS

250g / 9 oz / 1 ¼ cups basmati rice rinsed in several changes of cold water
100g / 3 ½ oz / ⅔ cup ham, chopped
handful mixed olives, stoned and chopped
4 spring onions (scallions), finely chopped
1 tbsp parsley, finely chopped
6 tbsp olive oil
1 tbsp red wine vinegar

Rice with Mozzarella

30

Mini balls of Mozzarella make a good addition, melting slightly in the warm salad.

31

SERVES 4

Stuffed Tomatoes

- Using a teaspoon, hollow out the tomatoes, discarding the seeds.
- Sprinkle the insides with a little salt and leave to drain upside down for 30 minutes.
- Meanwhile mix together the filling ingredients.
- Spoon the filling inside the tomatoes and serve cold.

PREPARATION TIME: 10 MINUTES

COOKING TIME: 40 MINUTES

INGREDIENTS

8 ripe beef tomatoes
salt

FOR THE FILLING:
250 g / 9 oz / 1 ⅓ cup Mascarpone
4 tbsp Parmesan, grated
4 tbsp flat leaf parsley, finely chopped
salt and pepper

Stuffed Tomatoes with Pesto

32

Stir 2 tbsp pesto into the filling ingredients.

Arancini

Arancini with Mozzarella

 34

Substitute a small cube of Mozzarella for the ratatouille

Arancini with Ricotta and Spinach

35

Substitute the ratatouille for 150 g / 5 oz Ricotta and 225 g / 8 oz spinach that have been mixed. Cook the same.

Arancini with Mushrooms and Peas

 36

Omit the ratatouille for 150 g / 5 oz / 2 cups chopped chanterelles and 200 g / 7 oz / 2 cups frozen, thawed peas.

PREPARATION TIME: 20 MINUTES

COOKING TIME: 10 MINUTES

INGREDIENTS

275g / 10 oz / 1 cup cooked arborio rice, cold
1 tbsp Parmesan, grated
4 tbsp cooked ratatouille
1 tbsp plain (all purpose) flour
1 egg, beaten
40g / 1 ½ oz / ⅓ cup breadcrumbs
Vegetable oil, for deep frying

- Stir the Parmesan through the risotto.
- Shape into equal balls, pushing a small tsp of ratatouille into the centre of each one and shaping the rice around it.
- Lay out the flour, egg and breadcrumbs on separate plates.
- Dip the risotto balls into the flour, then the egg, then the breadcrumbs. Use one hand and keep the other clean for ease.
- Heat the oil to 180°C / 400F or until a cube of bread sizzles when dropped in the oil. Fry the risotto balls until golden and crisp all over.
- Serve hot or warm.

37

SERVES 6

Fennel and Onion Confit

- Peel the onions, cut in half across the middle.
- Remove the base of the fennel and cut into quarters. Remove any hard woody core but try to leave the bulb intact.
- Heat the oil in a large pan then add the onions cut side down and the fennel quarters.
- Leave until they turn golden, then reduce the heat, add the herbs, stock and season. Cover and leave to cook gently for 30 minutes.
- Add the honey then cook for another 15 minutes.
- Adjust the seasoning and serve hot.

PREPARATION TIME: 10 MINUTES

COOKING TIME: 45 MINUTES

INGREDIENTS

6 onions
6 fennel bulbs
6 tbsp olive oil
150ml / 5 fl oz / 2/3 cup vegetable stock
3 bay leaves
1 sprig thyme
2 tbsp rosemary-flavoured honey

Meaty Confit

38

If serving with red meat, use beef stock or use chicken stock if serving with poultry. Both of these will give a very rich meaty flavour.

39

SERVES 4

Greens and Pasta Salad

- Cook the pasta in boiling salted water according to packet instructions.
- Drain and toss with olive oil.
- Meanwhile cut the courgette (zucchini) into small matchsticks and squeeze over a little lemon juice and salt to macerate.
- Finely chop the fennel and add to the courgette (zucchini), along with the celery and herbs and mix well.
- Once the pasta is cooked, toss with the vegetables and add more oil to lubricate.
- Season well and serve.

PREPARATION TIME: 20 MINUTES

COOKING TIME: 15 MINUTES

INGREDIENTS

400g / 14 oz / 3 ½ cups orechiette pasta
1 courgette (zucchini)
1 fennel bulb, root trimmed
2 celery stalks, finely chopped
1 tbsp mint, chopped
1 tbsp basil, chopped
110 ml / 4 fl. oz / ½ cup olive oil
1 lemon, juiced

Pasta Salad with Spinach

40

Add a handful baby spinach leaves at the last minute

41

MAKES 18

Ham and Mozzarella Muffins

- Preheat the oven to 220°C (180° fan) / 400F / gas 7.
- Tip the flour into a bowl and make a well in the centre.
- Whisk together the wet ingredients and pour into the flour. Mix together roughly until just about incorporated.
- Stir in the cheese, ham and rosemary.
- Spoon into a lined muffin tin, then bake for about 20 minutes until golden and cooked through at the centre.
- Leave to cool slightly before serving.

PREPARATION TIME: 15 MINUTES

COOKING TIME: 20 MINUTES

INGREDIENTS

500 g / 1 lb 2 oz / 3 ⅓ cups self-raising flour
80 g / 3 oz / ⅔ stick butter, melted
1 egg, beaten
250 ml / 9 fl. oz / 1 cup milk
100 g / 4 oz / ⅔ cup Mozzarella, cubed
100 g / 4 oz / ⅔ cup ham, diced
2 sprigs rosemary leaves, finely chopped

Italian-style Courgettes

42

SERVES 4

PREPARATION TIME: 15 MINUTES

COOKING TIME: 20 MINUTES

INGREDIENTS

4 courgettes (zucchini)
200g / 7 oz / 1 ⅓ cups Ricotta
1 tbsp parsley, finely chopped

1 tbsp basil, finely chopped
1 tbsp mint, finely chopped
2 tbsp olive oil
4 tbsp Parmesan, grated

- Preheat the oven to 200°C / 180° fan / 400F / gas 6.
- Slice the courgettes in half lengthways and scoop out the flesh, leaving the sides intact.
- Finely dice the flesh. Heat 2 tbsp oil in a pan and cook the courgette flesh until tender. Tip into a bowl and leave to cool.
- Once cool, stir into the ricotta, herbs and season well.
- Use a spoon to stuff the interiors of the courgettes, drizzle with oil and sprinkle over the Parmesan.
- Bake in the oven for about 20 minutes or until the courgettes are tender and bubbling.

Tricolore Pasta Salad

43

SERVES 4

PREPARATION TIME: 15 MINUTES

COOKING TIME: 20 MINUTES

INGREDIENTS

400 g / 14 oz / 3 ½ cups farfalle
300 g / 10 ½ oz / 2 cups cherry tomatoes

2 green peppers, roasted and cooled
1 ball buffalo mozzarella
1 tbsp basil, chopped
4 tbsp olive oil
2 tbsp red wine vinegar

- Cook the pasta in boiling salted water according to packet instructions.
- Drain and toss with olive oil.
- Meanwhile tip the tomatoes into a bowl with the peppers and drizzle with the olive oil, the vinegar and season.
- Toss the cooked pasta with the tomatoes and peppers, adding more oil if necessary to lubricate. Adjust the seasoning.
- Tear over the mozzarella and serve.

44

SERVES 4

Asparagus with Parmesan crust

- Steam the asparagus for 4-5 minutes until just tender to the point of a knife.
- Remove from the heat and leave to cool.
- Meanwhile blend the bread in a food processor to make breadcrumbs, adding the Parmesan as you go.
- Lay the asparagus on a baking sheet and sprinkle over the breadcrumbs and a little seasoning. Drizzle with oil.
- Flash under a hot grill until the crust turns golden.

PREPARATION TIME: 5 MINUTES

COOKING TIME: 8 MINUTES

INGREDIENTS

8 stalks asparagus, woody ends snapped off
2 thick slices of bread, crusts removed
3 tbsp Parmesan, grated
2 tbsp olive oil

Asparagus with Herb Crust 45

Add 1 tbsp finely chopped rosemary or thyme leaves to the breadcrumbs

46

SERVES 4

Italian Stuffed Galette

- Heat 1 tbsp butter in a pan and when foaming add the chopped tomatoes. Season with salt and pepper and cook until just tender, but not collapsed
- Heat the remaining butter in a separate pan and when foaming, add the eggs.
- Stir continuously until the eggs are nearly cooked and are thick and creamy.
- Stir in the ham and some seasoning.
- Spoon some egg and ham down the centre of each pancake, then roll up into a tube and place on a plate. Keep warm while you complete the remaining pancakes.
- Just before serving scatter with the tomatoes and basil.

PREPARATION TIME: 5 MINUTES

COOKING TIME: 15 MINUTES

INGREDIENTS

FOR THE FILLING:
4 tbsp butter
4 tomatoes, chopped
6 eggs, beaten
4 slices Parma ham, finely chopped
½ handful basil
8 buckwheat pancakes, warmed

Italian Galette with Cheese 47

Add 2-3 tbsp grated cheese of your choice to the eggs

48

MAKES 4

Stuffed Italian Peppers

PREPARATION TIME: 15 MINUTES

COOKING TIME: 35 MINUTES

INGREDIENTS

4 long green peppers
4 tomatoes
150g / 5 oz / 2/3 cup cream cheese
2 tbsp olive oil
1 tbsp parsley, finely chopped

- Preheat the oven to 200°C (180° fan) / 400F / gas 6.
- Cut the peppers in half then deseed and remove any white pith.
- Place in a roasting tray, drizzle with 1 tbsp oil and some seasoning before roasting for 20-25 minutes until they start to collapse.
- Plunge the tomatoes into boiling water for 20 seconds. Remove and peel away the skins.
- Cut the tomatoes in half and discard the seeds. Dice the flesh.
- Place the cream cheese in a bowl, add the tomato concasse and 1 tbsp olive oil and season. Mix well.
- Spoon the filling into the cavity of the peppers and return to the oven for 5-10 minutes.
- Serve warm with the parsley scattered over.

Olive Stuffed Peppers **49**

Add a handful of pitted, chopped black olives to the filling.

Blue Cheese Stuffed Peppers **50**

Add 100 g of blue cheese to give this recipe an extra strong flavour.

MAKES 20-24 51

Breadsticks

Cheese Breadsticks 52

Sprinkle some cheese on top of each bread stick before baking.

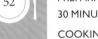

Garlic Breadsticks 53

Add 1 tsp of garlic powder and 1 tsp of dried parsley to the dough before kneading.

Pepper Breadsticks 54

Add 1 tsp of crushed black peppercorns to the dough before kneading.

PREPARATION TIME:
30 MINUTES + PROVING TIME

COOKING TIME: 15-20 MINUTES

INGREDIENTS

450 g / 1 lb / 3 cups white bread flour
1 x 7 g sachet dried yeast
1 ½ tsp salt
250 ml / 9 fl. oz / 1 cup lukewarm water
olive oil
sea salt

- Place the flour, yeast and salt in a bowl, then add the water a little at a time to form a dough.
- Bring the dough together with your hands and knead well for 10 minutes until smooth and elastic.
- Divide the mixture into about 20 equal portions then roll into sausage shapes. You can leave them like this or twist them.
- Place well spaced apart on floured baking sheets, cover with a damp tea towel and leave in a warm place for 30 minutes.
- Preheat the oven to 200°C (180° fan) / 400F / gas 6.
- Brush with the olive oil and sprinkle with a little sea salt, then bake for about 15-20 minutes or until cooked.
- Serve with dips or wrapped in Parma ham.

55

SERVES 4-6

Parmesan Soup

PREPARATION TIME: 5 MINUTES

COOKING TIME: 15 MINUTES

....

INGREDIENTS

1.5 l / 2 pints 12 fl. oz / 6 cups chicken stock
2 eggs
2 tbsp Parmesan cheese, grated
bunch basil leaves
250 g / 9 oz / 2 cups spinach leaves, shredded
salt and pepper
nutmeg

- Bring the chicken stock to the boil in a pan.
- Whisk together the eggs, Parmesan and basil until completely blended.
- Lower the heat. Whisking constantly in a figure of eight motion, stir the egg mixture into the stock a little at a time until all is incorporated.
- Leave to simmer very gently for about 5 minutes until thickened.
- Stir through the spinach and a little grated nutmeg.
- Adjust the seasoning before serving.

Bready Parmesan Soup

56

To make this more substantial, toast some slices of ciabatta and place in the bottom of the bowl before ladling the soup over.

57

SERVES 4

Stuffed Tomatoes and Bell Peppers

PREPARATION TIME: 40 MINUTES

COOKING TIME: 30 MINUTES

....

INGREDIENTS

4 ripe beef tomatoes
4 peppers
1 tbsp olive oil
1 onion, peeled and finely chopped
2 cloves garlic, finely chopped
300g / 10 ½ oz / 2 cups minced beef
1 tbsp rosemary leaves, finely chopped
2 tbsp tomato puree
2 tbsp Parmesan, grated

- Using a teaspoon, hollow out the tomatoes, discarding the seeds.
- Sprinkle the insides with a little salt and leave to drain.
- Cut the tops off the peppers, setting them aside, and hollow out the insides.
- Meanwhile fry the onion and garlic in the oil. Add the beef and rosemary, increase the heat and fry briskly. Season with salt and pepper.
- Stir in the tomato puree and a cup of water and leave to simmer until the water is absorbed. Stir in the Parmesan and leave to cool a little.
- Preheat the oven to 200°C (180° fan) / 400F / gas 6.
- Fill the tomatoes and peppers with the beef mixture and place in a roasting tin.
- Drizzle with olive oil and bake in the oven for about 30 minutes or until they are soft but retaining their shape.
- Serve hot or warm with salad.

Shrimp Stuffed Tomatoes and Bell Peppers

58

Try using prawns (shrimps) instead of the beef for seafood lovers.

SERVES 4

Veal Piccata with Cantal Cheese

- Place the escalopes between 2 slices of film and bat out until very thin with a rolling pin.
- Cut the cheese into 12 slices.
- Lay a veal escalope out on the surface, season it, then place a slice of cheese and 2 sage leaves on top. Top this with a slice of ham.
- Roll the escalope up and secure with a toothpick. Repeat for all the veal slices.
- Heat the oil in a pan, then add the rolled-up escalopes and garlic and cook until golden all over. This should take about 10 minutes.
- Serve warm with a salad and sage leaves to decorate.

PREPARATION TIME: 10 MINUTES

COOKING TIME: 10 MINUTES

INGREDIENTS

12 veal escalopes, around 80 g / 3 oz each
250 g / 9 oz / 2 cups Cantal cheese
12 thin slices cured ham
3 sprigs sage
4 tbsp olive oil
salt and pepper

Veal Piccata with Emmental Cheese

Swap the sage for fresh basil leaves and the Cantal cheese for Emmental.

SERVES 4

Griddled Aubergine with Pesto

- Slice the aubergines across into 1cm / ½" thick pieces.
- Brush each slice with olive oil and season.
- Preheat a griddle pan or barbecue until very hot. Lay the aubergine slices over the heat and griddle on each side until charred and tender.
- Spoon the pesto over the aubergines to serve.

PREPARATION TIME: 5 MINUTES

COOKING TIME: 10 MINUTES

INGREDIENTS

2 aubergines
2 tbsp olive oil
6 tbsp pesto

Cheesy Aubergines with Pesto

After spooning over the pesto, lay on slices of mozzarella and grill till oozing.

SERVES 4

Polenta with Ham Canapés

Polenta with Fig Canapés

64

Wrap the ham around half a fresh fig before placing on the polenta.

Chicken and Parmesan Canapés

65

Replace the Polenta and ham with 100 g / 3.5 oz diced chicken which has been flash fried in 1 tsp olive oil until white, and 25 g / 1 oz Parmesan shavings.

Black Olive with Sundried Tomato

66

Replace the Polenta and ham with 10-12 pitted black olives and 10-12 sundried tomatoes.

PREPARATION TIME: 35 MINUTES

COOKING TIME: 45 MINUTES

INGREDIENTS

200g / 7 oz / 1 cup polenta
1.5 l / 2 pints 12 fl. oz / 6 cups water
Parma ham slices
Olive oil

- Whisk the polenta slowly into a large pan of boiling salted water.
- As soon as it begins to boil, stir every 5 minutes, ensuring you push the spoon down into the sides of the pan.
- Cook for about 45 minutes until it begins to have the consistency of mashed potato. Season with salt and pepper.
- Oil a tray and tip the polenta out onto to it. Spread the polenta to about 2.5cm / 1" thick.
- Leave the polenta to cool for about 30 minutes and then cut circles out 5cm / 2" in diameter.
- Meanwhile, cut the Parma ham into pieces and arrange on the polenta circles. Secure with a toothpick and drizzle with olive oil before serving.

67

SERVES 4

Pork Piccata

- Preheat the oven to 200°C (180 ° fan) / 400F / gas 6.
- Open the pork tenderloin out by inserting your knife to about halfway into the fillet, then cutting along the length then opening it out like a book.
- Place between 2 sheets of film (plastic wrap) and bat out gently with a rolling pin until a little thinner and more even.
- Lay the cheese and chorizo on top, then roll up the tenderloin to form a fat sausage. Secure with toothpicks.
- Heat the olive oil in an ovenproof pan and sear the pork on all sides until golden. Add the white wine if using (it makes a very nice sauce) and place in the oven for about 12-15 minutes until the pork is just cooked and the cheese is oozing.
- Slice into thick pieces to serve. Reduce the juices in the pan until syrupy and pour over the pork piccata.

PREPARATION TIME: 15 MINUTES

COOKING TIME: 12 MINUTES

INGREDIENTS

900 g / 2 lb pork tenderloin
100 g / 4 oz / 1 cup Tomme cheese
12 thin slices chorizo sausage
2 tbsp olive oil
120ml / 4 ½ fl oz / ½ cup dry white wine

Pork Piccata with Rosemary

 68

Secure the pork with rosemary sprigs for a boost of flavour.

69

SERVES 4

Italian-style Sautéed Asparagus

- Heat the oil in the pan and add the asparagus.
- Cook briskly for 3 minutes then add the garlic and salt and pepper.
- Sauté until the spears are starting to caramelise and become tender – about 10 minutes.
- To serve, drizzle with oil and lemon juice, then scatter over the Parmesan and pine nuts.

PREPARATION TIME: 5 MINUTES

COOKING TIME: 10 MINUTES

INGREDIENTS

12 asparagus spears, trimmed
olive oil
2 cloves garlic, finely sliced
½ lemon, juiced
Olive oil, to serve
2 tbsp Parmesan shavings to serve
1 tbsp pine nuts, lightly toasted

Italian-style Sautéed Asparagus with Gorgonzola

 70

Add a handful crumbled Gorgonzola at the end of cooking to melt over.

71
SERVES 6

Primavera

PREPARATION TIME: 30 MINUTES

COOKING TIME: 25 MINUTES

INGREDIENTS

400 g /14 oz / 3 ½ cups penne pasta
12 slices Coppa ham
12 small balls mozzarella
1 bunch asparagus
6 sprigs thyme
olive oil
salt and pepper

- Steam the asparagus for about 10 minutes or until tender.
- Meanwhile, cut the mozzarella balls in half.
- Wash and pick the thyme leaves.
- Heat the grill.
- Place the asparagus on foil and drizzle with olive oil. Season and place under the grill for about 5 minutes, watching them carefully, until lightly charred.
- Heat a frying pan and sear the ham until crisp.
- Cook the pasta in boiling salted water according to packet instructions. Drain and drizzle with oil and season.
- Spoon onto a plate, then top with the asparagus, Coppa ham and mozzarella, drizzle with more oil and sprinkle over the thyme.

Courgette Primavera 72

Grill thin strips of courgette alongside the asparagus.

73
SERVES 4

Pappardelle with Ham

PREPARATION TIME: 15 MINUTES

COOKING TIME: 10 MINUTES

INGREDIENTS

400 g / 14 oz / 3 ½ cups pappardelle pasta
6 slices of cured ham, such as Parma
2 bunches rocket
60 g / 2 oz / ½ stick cup butter
110 g / 4 oz / 1 cup Parmesan, grated
250 ml / 9 fl. oz / 1 cup crème fraiche
salt and pepper

- Cook the pasta in a large pan of boiling salted water until al dente or just tender.
- Drain and toss with a little olive oil to prevent sticking.
- Cut the cured ham in half lengthways.
- Roughly chop the rocket.
- Heat the butter in a pan, add the pasta and stir. Sprinkle over the Parmesan then add the crème fraiche. Season and mix well.
- Divide the pasta between 4 bowls and then lay the ham and rocket on top before serving.

Pappardelle with Mushrooms 74

Substitute the ham with handful of mushrooms fried in the butter before adding the pasta.

75

SERVES 6

Italian Salad with Soft-boiled Egg Dressing

Italian Salad with Parma Ham

76

You could add chopped Parma ham for meat lovers.

Italian Salad with Olives

77

Replace the peppers with black olives.

Italian Salad with Pecorino

78

Substitute the Parmesan with Pecorino for a sharper taste.

PREPARATION TIME: 30 MINUTES

COOKING TIME: 25 MINUTES

INGREDIENTS

2 red peppers
2 yellow peppers
Parmesan, to shave
120g / 4 ½ oz / ⅔ cup sun-dried tomatoes
175g / 6 oz / ¾ cup rocket (arugula) leaves
6 eggs
2 tbsp olive oil
2 tbsp balsamic vinegar
3 thick slices granary bread, cut in half

- Cut the peppers in half and discard the seeds and white pith.
- Lay on a baking sheet and grill until completely blackened. Remove from the heat, place in a plastic bag and leave to cool.
- Peel the skin away from the peppers and roughly chop the flesh.
- Place in a bowl with the rocket, tomatoes and some shaved Parmesan and set aside.
- Cook the eggs in boiling water for 6 minutes. Remove, leave to cool a little then peel away the shell.
- Dress the salad with the olive oil and balsamic vinegar. Season well.
- Serve the salad with the egg just broken in half on top and the bread alongside.

Mini Pizza Appetisers

PREPARATION TIME:
45 MINUTES + PROVING TIME

COOKING TIME: 8-10 MINUTES

INGREDIENTS

FOR THE PIZZA DOUGH:
400 g / 14 oz / 2 ⅔ cups strong white
bread flour
100 g / 3 ½ oz / ⅔ cup fine ground
semolina flour
½ tbsp salt
1 x 7 g sachet dried yeast
½ tbsp caster (superfine) sugar
350 ml / 12 fl. oz / 1 ⅖ cup lukewarm
water

FOR THE TOPPING:
bottled passata
anchovies
black olives, stoned
small handful rocket leaves
2 tbsp pine kernels
basil, to garnish

- Pour the flour and salt into a bowl and make a well in the centre.
- Add the yeast and sugar to the water, mix with a fork and leave for a few minutes. Pour into the well.
- Bring in the flour from around the insides and mix into the water. When it starts coming together, use your hands and pat it into a ball.
- Knead the dough for 10 minutes. Flour the dough, cover with film and leave to rest for 30 minutes.
- Preheat the oven to 240°C (220° fan) / 475F / gas 9. Flour the surface, tear off a piece of dough and roll into a rough rectangle or square.
- Dust each one with a little flour and lay out on the surface. Spread passata on each one, then top with olives, anchovies and rocket.
- Sprinkle with pine kernels and place on a baking sheet. Bake for 8-10 minutes until golden.

Mini Taleggio Pizza Appetisers

80

Add a little thinly-sliced Taleggio cheese to the toppings before baking.

Aubergine and Mozzarella Sandwiches

PREPARATION TIME: 20 MINUTES

COOKING TIME: 5 MINUTES

INGREDIENTS

1 ciabatta loaf, ready baked
extra virgin olive oil
2 cloves of garlic, halved
4 tbsp olive oil
1 aubergine, thinly sliced
salt
4 ripe tomatoes, thickly sliced
pinch dried red chilli flakes
150 g / 5 oz / 1 cup Mozzarella, thinly
sliced
dried oregano

- Slice the ciabatta in half horizontally and toast under a hot grill until crunchy.
- Rub with garlic and drizzle with olive oil.
- Heat the oil in a pan and fry the aubergine rounds in batches until golden and tender. Sprinkle with a little salt and leave to drain on kitchen paper as you cook.
- Place the tomato slices on the toasted ciabatta and press down lightly.
- Top with the aubergine slices. Sprinkle with dried chilli if desired.
- Add the mozzarella and a sprinkle of oregano, drizzle with a little oil and brown under the grill till golden and bubbling.

Anchovy and Mozzarella Sandwiches

82

Add 2 anchovies in the oil before adding the aubergine to add a burst of deep flavour.

83

SERVES 4

Garlic Bread

- Slice the baguettes on a diagonal to get elongated slices.
- Mix the butter thoroughly with the garlic and parsley.
- Spread the butter thickly onto the bread.
- Top with slices of cheese and flash under a hot grill until bubbling and golden.

PREPARATION TIME 10 MINS

COOKING TIME 45 MINS

INGREDIENTS

2 baguettes
120g / 4 oz / 1 stick butter, softened
4 cloves garlic, crushed
1 tbsp parsley, finely chopped
225 g / 8 oz / 2 cups Fontina

Cheesy Baguettes

84

If you prefer, keep the baguettes whole, partly slice through all the way along and fill the gaps with the butter and grate the cheese over. Wrap in foil and bake for 20 minutes.

85

SERVES 8

Sun-dried Tomato Cake

- Preheat oven to 190°C / 375F / gas 5.
- Whisk the eggs and sugar together until pale and thick.
- Sieve the flours, baking powder and salt into a bowl, then fold into the eggs.
- Stir in the sour cream and oil until incorporated.
- Stir in the tomatoes, paprika and thyme leaves.
- Grease and line four mini-loaf tins, then divide the mixture equally between them.
- Bake in the oven for about 40 minutes until a skewer inserted into the middle comes out clean.
- Remove to a wire rack and allow to cool.

PREPARATION TIME: 25 MINUTES

COOKING TIME: 40 MINUTES

INGREDIENTS

3 eggs
1 tsp sugar
225g /8 oz / 1 ½ cup plain (all purpose) flour
55 g / 2 oz / ⅓ cup potato flour
2 tsp baking (soda) powder
½ tsp salt
6 tbsp olive oil
2 tbsp sour cream
275 g / 10 oz / 1 ¾ cups sun-dried tomatoes, chopped
1 tsp paprika
1 tbsp thyme leaves, finely chopped

Courgette cake

86

For an extra zesty twist on this recipe, substitute the lemon for a lime. tute the lemon for a lime. Forzeston this recipe, substitute.

87

SERVES 4

Carrots with Parmesan

PREPARATION TIME: 5 MINUTES

COOKING TIME: 30 MINUTES

INGREDIENTS

8 carrots, peeled
3 tbsp olive oil
1 tbsp rosemary leaves, finely chopped
8 tbsp Parmesan, grated

- Preheat the oven to 200°C (180° fan) / 400F / gas 6.
- Cut the carrots into cork-length pieces and place in a roasting tin.
- Toss with oil, seasoning and rosemary and roast in the oven for 15-20 minutes until they start to soften and colour.
- Toss with the Parmesan, return to the oven and roast for a further 5-10 minutes until golden and caramelised.
- Serve hot.

Carrots with Pecorino

88

Use the same amount of Pecorino cheese for a lemony flavour

89

MAKES 2

Rosemary focaccia

PREPARATION TIME:
2 HOURS 40 MINUTES

COOKING TIME: 20 MINUTES

INGREDIENTS

750g / 1 lb 10 oz / 5 cups '00' flour (Italian super-white flour)
½ tsp salt
2 tsp fast-action dried yeast
150 ml / 5 fl. oz / ⅔ cup olive oil
450 ml / 16 fl. oz / 2 cups lukewarm water
Handful rosemary leaves

- Sift the flour and salt into a bowl and make a well in the centre. Pour 50ml of the oil into the flour, add the yeast and rub together with your fingers.
- Pour in about 3/4 of the water and mix until the dough comes together. Tip the dough onto a floured surface and knead for 10 minutes until smooth and elastic.
- Place in a lightly oiled bowl, cover withfilm and leave to rise in a warm place for 1 hour 30 minutes.
- Take the dough out, punch out the air and divide in to two balls. Roll into 2 circles and place in 2 lightly oiled pizza pans. Cover with film and leave for 30 minutes.
- Preheat the oven to 200°C (180° fan) / 400F / gas 6. Push your fingertips into the dough to make dimples.
- Drizzle with oil so that the dimples fill up. Top with sprigs of rosemary. Sprinkle with salt.
- Spray with water and bake for 20 minutes until golden.
- Drizzle with the remaining oil and transfer to a wire rack to cool before serving.

Basil Focaccia

90

Substitute the rosemary for basil.

MAKES 3-4

Pumpkin and Tomato Pizzas

Pumpkin and Tomato Pizza with Passata

92

Spread 1 tbsp of passata over the base of each pizza before the toppings for a stronger tomato flavour.

Butternut Squash Pizzas

93

Replace the same amount of pumpkin with butternut squash.

Pumpkin Seed Tomato Pizzas

94

Drizzle the de-seeded pumpkin seeds on the top of the pizza before placing in the oven.

PREPARATION TIME:
I HOUR 20 MINUTES

COOKING TIME: 30 MINUTES

INGREDIENTS

FOR THE PIZZA DOUGH
400 g / 14 oz / 2 ⅔ cups strong white bread flour
100 g / 3 ½ oz / ⅔ cup fine ground semolina flour
½ tbsp salt
½ tbsp dried yeast
½ tbsp caster (superfine) sugar
350ml / 12 fl. oz / 1 ⅖ cups lukewarm water

FOR THE TOPPING
1 butternut squash, halved and deseeded
1 tbsp olive oil
20 cherry tomatoes, halved
2 balls mozzarella
Handful basil leaves

- To make the pizza, pour the flours and salt into a bowl and make a well in the centre, add the yeast and sugar to the water, mix with a fork and leave for a few minutes.
- Bring in all the flour, working your way towards the outer edges, mixing well.
- When it starts to come together, use your hands and pat it into a ball.
- Knead the dough for around 10 minutes until the dough is smooth and elastic, cover with film (plastic wrap) and leave to rest for 30 minutes.
- Preheat the oven to 240°C (220° fan) / 475F / gas 9.
- Cut the butternut squash into small chunks and roast for about 20 minutes in the oven with the olive oil until tender and caramelised.
- Roll the pizzas out about 30 minutes before you want to cook them. Flour the surface, tear off a piece of dough and roll into a rough circle about 1cm / ½" thick.
- Top each pizza with some of the butternut squash, halved tomatoes and small pieces of mozzarella.
- Place either directly on the bars of the oven or on a preheated baking sheet for 8-10 minutes until golden and crisp.
- Sprinkle with basil leaves before serving.

31

95

SERVES 4

Avocado, Tomato and Feta

Avocado with Mozzarella

96

Substitute the feta with buffalo mozzarella for a mouth-watering twist.

Avocado with Crabmeat

97

Substitute the feta for 100 g / 3 ½ oz crab meat.

Avocado with Tomato and Gorgonzola

98

Replace the feta for the same weight in Gorgonzola.

PREPARATION TIME: 20 MINUTES

COOKING TIME: N/A

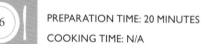

INGREDIENTS

2-3 ripe vine grown tomatoes
extra virgin olive oil
100 g / 3 ½ oz / ⅔ cup feta cheese
2 tbsp black olives, stoned
basil leaves
salt and pepper
2 ripe avocados
juice of ½ lemon, optional

- Finely chop the tomatoes and place in a bowl. Season and drizzle with olive oil then leave to marinate for 10 minutes.
- Dice the feta into small chunks, then add to the tomatoes, along with the olives. Tear up the basil leaves and add these too. Season to taste.
- Cut the avocados in half when ready to serve and remove the stones.
- Squeeze over a little lemon to prevent discolouring.
- Fill the cavity in each avocado with the tomato and feta salad and serve.

99
SERVES 4

Italian Rustic Tomato Soup

- Heat the oil in a pan and sweat the onion, carrot and celery without colouring.
- Add the garlic and cook for 2 minutes until soft.
- Add the courgettes and potatoes, stir well and leave to soften for a 5-10 minutes, then add the ham.
- Pour in the tomatoes, crumble in a little of the chilli, then stir in the stock.
- Bring to a simmer and leave to cook until the vegetables are tender – about 20 minutes.
- Taste and adjust the seasoning if necessary, adding chilli if desired.
- Roughly mash the vegetables with a potato masher or pulse in a liquidiser.
- Serve drizzled with olive oil.

Vegetarian Soup
100
Omit the ham and substitute the chicken stock with vegetable stock, for a vegetarian alternative.

PREPARATION TIME: 15 MINUTES
COOKING TIME: 30-35 MINUTES

INGREDIENTS

2 tbsp olive oil
1 onion, peeled and chopped
1 carrot, peeled and finely chopped
1 celery stalk, finely chopped
2 cloves of garlic, chopped
1 courgette, finely chopped
2 potatoes, peeled and finely chopped
2 slices Parma ham, chopped
400 g / 14 oz / 2 cups canned chopped tomatoes
1 dried red chilli, chopped
1 l / 1 pint 16 fl. oz / 4 cups chicken stock
salt and pepper
extra virgin olive oil

101
SERVES 6

Mushroom Ravioli

- Place the flour in a bowl and make a well in the centre. Crack the eggs into the well.
- Beat the eggs, then draw in the flour until the dough comes together. Knead the dough for 5 minutes. Cover with film and rest for 30 minutes in the refrigerator.
- Heat the butter and sweat the onion and mushrooms. Stir in the Parmesan and parsley and season.
- Using a pasta machine, roll the dough into sheets 2 mm thick and 10 cm wide. Lay on a floured surface.
- Place 1 tsp of filling in the middle of the sheet at one end. Repeat all the way along at 5cm intervals and then brush a little water in a circle, around each filling.
- Place another sheet of pasta on top, then push the sheets together and around each mound of filling.
- Cut the ravioli into shapes. Bring a large pan of salted water to the boil and cook for 3-4 minutes. Remove carefully with a slotted spoon then toss with more butter and Parmesan to serve.

Ricotta and Mushroom Ravioli
102
Use 150 g / 5 oz / 1 cup ricotta in the filling for a creamier texture.

PREPARATION TIME: 45 MINUTES - 1 HOUR + RESTING TIME
COOKING TIME: 3 MINUTES

INGREDIENTS

FOR THE PASTA:
500 g / 1 lb 2 oz / 3 ⅓ cups '00' flour
6 eggs

FOR THE FILLING:
3 tbsp butter
200 g / 7 oz / 2 ⅔ cup wild mushrooms, brushed clean
150 g / 5 oz / 2 cups flat mushrooms, finely chopped
½ onion, peeled and finely chopped
2 tbsp Parmesan, grated
1 tbsp flat leaf parsley, finely chopped
salt and pepper

GARNISH
butter
Parmesan, grated

103

SERVES 4

Polenta Galettes

PREPARATION TIME:

5 MINUTES + COOLING TIME

COOKING TIME: 45 MINUTES

INGREDIENTS

200 g / 7 oz / 1 cup polenta
1.5 l / 2 pints 12 fl. oz / 6 cups water
130 g / 4 ½ oz / 1 ¼ cups Parmesan, grated

- Whisk the polenta slowly into a large pan of boiling salted water.
- As soon as it begins to boil, cover loosely with a lid and turn the heat down as low as possible.
- When it begins to thicken, stir well every 5 minutes or so, ensuring you push the spoon down into the sides of the pan.
- Cook for about 45 minutes until it begins to have the consistency of mashed potato. Season generously and stir in the Parmesan.
- Oil a tray and tip the polenta out onto to it. Spread the polenta to about 2.5 cm thick.
- Leave the polenta to cool for about 30 minutes and then cut circles out 5 cm in diameter. Top with anything you fancy.

Polenta and Gorgonzola Galettes

104

Use Gorgonzola for a stronger flavour than the Parmesan.

105

MAKES 12

Italian Gougeres

PREPARATION TIME 10 MINS

COOKING TIME 45 MINS

INGREDIENTS

110g / 4 oz / ⅔ cup plain (all-purpose) flour
½ tsp salt
½ tsp black pepper
½ tsp dried oregano
Pinch Cayenne pepper
250ml / 9 fl oz / 1 cup milk
125g / 4 ½ oz / 1 ⅙ sticks butter, cubed
6 eggs, 1 separated
2 tbsp Parmesan, grated
4 tbsp Gruyere, grated
2 tbsp milk
4 tomatoes, sliced
handful of black olives, stoned and sliced
½ bunch basil leaves, chopped

- Preheat the oven to 220°C (200° fan) / 450F / gas 7.
- Place the flour in a bowl with the salt, pepper, oregano and Cayenne.
- Add the milk and butter to a large pan and bring to the boil. When the butter melts, reduce the heat and tip in the seasoned flour.
- Stir quickly and vigorously with a wooden spoon, beating until the dough starts to come away from the sides of the pan and form a ball.
- Remove the pan from the heat and tip into a large mixer bowl. Beat at a medium speed for 1 minute, then the eggs one at a time, beating until each one is absorbed before adding the next.
- Beat in the cheeses.
- Fill a piping bag with the mixture and use to pipe onto ungreased baking trays.
- Lightly press a tomato slice, a few chopped olives and basil into the centre of each one.
- Whisk the remaining egg yolk with the milk and lightly brush the gougeres.
- Bake for about 10 minutes, then reduce the heat to 150°C / 300F / gas 2 and bake for a further 15 minutes, or until golden brown.
- Cool on wire racks before serving.

106

MAKES 2

Olive Focaccia

- Sift the flour and salt into a bowl and make a well in the centre. Pour 2 tbsp of the oil into the flour, add the yeast and rub together with your fingers.
- Pour in about 3/4 of the water and mix until the dough comes together. Tip the dough onto a floured surface and knead for 10 minutes until smooth and elastic.
- Place in a lightly oiled bowl, cover with film and leave to rise in a warm place for 1 hour 30 minutes.
- Take the dough out and punch out the air. Work the olives into the dough. Divide into two balls.
- Roll into 2 circles and place in 2 lightly oiled pizza pans. Cover with film and leave to rise for 30 minutes.
- Preheat the oven to 200°C (180° fan) / 400F / gas 6. Uncover the dough and push your fingertips in to make deep dimples. Drizzle with oil so that the dimples fill up. Top with sprigs of rosemary. Sprinkle with salt.
- Spray with water and bake for 20 minutes. Drizzle with oil and transfer to a wire rack to cool before serving.

PREPARATION TIME:
2 HOURS 40 MINUTES

COOKING TIME: 20 MINUTES

INGREDIENTS

750g / 1 lb 10 oz / 5 cups '00' flour
(Italian super-white flour)
½ tsp salt
2 tsp fast-action dried yeast
150ml / 5 fl oz / 2/3 cup olive oil
450ml / 16 fl. oz / 1 ⅘ cups
lukewarm water
200g / 7 oz / 1 ⅓ cups mixed olives,
pitted and chopped
handful rosemary leaves

Olive and Chilli Focaccia

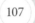
107

Add a finely chopped red chilli to the mix for a spicy kick.

108

SERVES 4

Polenta and Olive Chips

- Whisk the polenta slowly into a large pan of boiling salted water.
- As soon as it begins to boil stir every 5 minutes, ensuring you push the spoon down into the sides of the pan.
- Cook for about 45 minutes until it begins to have the consistency of mashed potato. Season generously and stir in the Parmesan and olives.
- Oil a tray and tip the polenta out onto to it. Spread the polenta to about 2.5cm thick
- Leave the polenta to cool for about 30 minutes, then cut into chip shapes when firm.
- Heat the oil to 180°C / 400F or until a cube of bread sizzles when dropped in the oil, deep fry the polenta chips in batches until golden and crisp.
- Drain on kitchen paper and sprinkle with salt before serving.

PREPARATION TIME: 35 MINUTES

COOKING TIME: 55 MINUTES

INGREDIENTS

200g / 7 oz / 1 cup polenta
1.5 l / 2 pints 12 fl. oz / 6 cups water
130g / 4 ½ oz / 1 ¼ cups Parmesan,
grated
2 handfuls black olives, stoned and
chopped
Oil for deep frying

Herby Polenta Chips

109

Add 1 tsp finely chopped rosemary to the polenta.

110

SERVES 6

Courgette, Feta and Tomato Bread

Courgette, Mozzarella and Tomato (Bread)

111

Replace the feta with 100 g / 4 oz / ⅔ cup of mozzarella and cook the same.

Courgette, Feta and Rosemary (Bread)

112

Substitute the thyme with rosemary.

Aubergine, Feta and Tomato (Bread)

113

Substitute the courgette with finely diced aubergine (eggplant).

PREPARATION TIME: 30 MINUTES

COOKING TIME: 35 MINUTES

....

INGREDIENTS

8 eggs
1 tbsp crème fraiche
2 courgettes (zucchini), finely diced
Handful sundried tomatoes, finely chopped
100g / 4 oz / ⅔ cup feta cheese, cubed
6 sprigs thyme
2 tbsp olive oil

- Preheat the oven to 180°C (160° fan) / 350F / gas 4.
- Beat the eggs with the crème fraiche in a large bowl.
- Add the courgettes (zucchini), tomatoes, feta, thyme leaves and season then mix together carefully.
- Oil a large frying pan, then pour the mixture in and bake for about 35 minutes until puffed and golden. The egg should be cooked through.
- Cut into squares and serve warm or cold.

114

SERVES 6

Scallop Carpaccio

- Peel and stone the avocados.
- Cut into pieces and place in a food processor with the lime juice.
- Peel and chop the onion and garlic and add to the avocados. Season and whizz to a smooth puree.
- Spoon into a bowl and cover with film, then refrigerate.
- Clean and pat dry the scallops. Slice horizontally into fine slices and place on a plate in a single layer.
- Finely chop the basil then place in a bowl with the oil and lemon.
- Use most of this to dress the scallops. Season, cover with film and refrigerate the scallops for 30 minutes.
- Finely dice the courgettes.
- Spoon the avocado puree onto plates. Alternate the scallops with courgette, then drizzle over the remaining oil mixture.

PREPARATION TIME: 50 MINUTES

INGREDIENTS

18 scallops, cleaned
4 tbsp olive oil
juice of 1 lemon
6 sprigs basil
3 small courgettes (zucchinis)
salt and pepper

FOR THE AVOCADO PUREE:

3 ripe avocados
1 onion
1 clove of garlic
juice of 1 lime
salt and pepper

Scallop and Chilli Carpaccio

115

Add a pinch of dried chilli flakes to the scallop dressing.

116

SERVES 6

Veal Piccata with Courgettes

- Cut the courgettes into strips and steam for 5 minutes.
- Place the veal escalopes between 2 sheets of cling film and pound with a rolling pin until thin.
- Heat the butter in a pan until foaming, then sear the escalopes on each side for 2 minutes.
- Season, add the lemon juice and increase the heat to reduce the liquid to a syrup. Pour over the escalopes.
- Cut each escalope into 6 equal triangles.
- Thread the escalopes onto a skewer, alternating with the courgettes, three to each skewer. Cover with foil to keep warm.
- Add the mascarpone to the pan and deglaze. Season and pour in any resting juices from the veal.
- Pour this mixture over the veal skewers and serve hot.

PREPARATION TIME: I5 MINUTES

COOKING TIME: I0 MINUTES

INGREDIENTS

4 courgettes
6 veal escalopes
60 g / 2 oz / ½ stick butter
1 lemon, juiced
250 g / 9 oz / 1 ⅔ cups Mascarpone
salt and pepper

Veal Piccata with Fennel

117

Replace the courgette with fine slices of fennel, cooked in the same manner.

118

MAKES 40 Crostini

PREPARATION TIME:
30-40 MINUTES

COOKING TIME: 8 MINUTES

INGREDIENTS

1 ficelle
olive oil
tapenade
20 sun-blush tomato halves
10 black olives, stoned and halved
150g / 5 oz / 2/3 cup mozzarella
1 jar roasted peppers
1 jar artichoke hearts
10 slices Parma ham

- Preheat the oven to 180°C (160° fan) / 350F / gas 5. Slice the ficelle into rounds, about 1cm thick.
- Dab each one with a little oil and bake in the oven until lightly golden and crisp , for about 8 minutes.
- For the first topping, spread a little tapenade thinly on a crostini. Press the tomato down and then top with the mozzarella and olive half.
- For the second topping, dab a little of the pepper oil from the jar on the crostini.
- Wrap a small piece of roasted pepper and artichoke in half a slice of ham and then place it on the crostini.
- Serve at room temperature.

Crostini with Ricotta and Peach

119

Replace the mozzarella with 150g / 5 oz / 2/3 cup ricotta cheese, and slice 1 ripe peach, placing on the Parma ham.

120

SERVES 4 Vegetable and Cod Minestrone

PREPARATION TIME: 20 MINUTES

COOKING TIME: I HOUR

INGREDIENTS

1 tbsp olive oil
70 g / 2 ¾ oz / ⅓ cup pancetta or smoked streaky bacon, chopped
1 onion, peeled and finely chopped
1 carrot, peeled and finely chopped
2 celery stalks, finely chopped
2 potatoes, peeled and finely chopped
2 tomatoes, finely chopped
1 L / 2 ½ pints / 5 cups chicken stock
60 g / 1 ½ oz / ¼ cup macaroni pasta
40 g / 1 oz frozen peas
1 courgette, finely chopped
400g / 13 ½ oz / 1 ½ cups cod loin
salt and pepper
extra virgin olive oil

- Heat the olive oil in a pan and cook the pancetta until the fat runs and it starts to turn golden.
- Add the onion, carrot and celery and cook until softened and translucent.
- Continue to add the potatoes and tomatoes and cook for a few minutes.
- Add the stock and simmer for 30 minutes until all the vegetables are tender.
- Once simmered, add the pasta and cook for a further 20 minutes.
- Finish with adding the peas, courgette and gently lower the fish into the soup and cook for another 10 minutes.
- Ladle into bowls to serve, drizzled with oil.

Vegetable Hake Minestrone

121

Substitute the cod loin for hake fish instead and cook the same.

122
SERVES 4

Turkey Saltimbocca with Ricotta

- Finely chop the herbs and watercress. Mix together with the ricotta and season with salt and pepper.
- Place the escalopes between 2 sheets of film (plastic wrap) and bat out till quite thin.
- Divide the olive oil between 2 pans, heat and then and sear the escalopes for 2 minutes on each side.
- Remove from the heat, then spread on a little of the ricotta mix. Lay over a slice of braesola and a basil leaf, then roll up and secure with a toothpick.
- Halve the tomatoes and return to the pan with the escalopes. Cover with a lid and cook for another 3 minutes until the tomatoes have collapsed and the turkey is cooked through.
- Serve 2 per person with the tomatoes.

PREPARATION TIME: 20 MINUTES

COOKING TIME: 15 MINUTES

INGREDIENTS

1 handful basil
1 handful watercress
1 handful chives
100g / 3 ½ oz / ½ cup ricotta
4 turkey escalopes
8 slices braesola (dry-cured beef)
5 tbsp olive oil
24 cherry tomatoes

Turkey Saltimbocca with Mascarpone

123

Use mascarpone or cubed Fontina instead of ricotta

124
SERVES 4-6

Tomatoes with Ratatouille

- Heat half the oil in a large pan and add the aubergine (eggplant) and pepper and cook for 10 minutes.
- Then add the courgettes (zucchini), stir well, reduce the heat and cook for a further 10 minutes.
- Finally, add the tomatoes, season, cover and cook for 15 minutes.
- Cut the olives into rounds and then add to the pan with the basil.
- Preheat the oven to 210°C (190° fan) / 420F / gas 7.
- Take the tops off the tomatoes and hollow out with a teaspoon.
- Place in a roasting tin and fill each one with ratatoutille. Place the tops back on, drizzle with the rest of the oil and cook in the oven for about 25 minutes.
- Serve hot or warm.

PREPARATION TIME: 35 MINUTES

COOKING TIME: I HOUR

INGREDIENTS

FOR THE RATATOUILLE:
8 tbsp olive oil
2 tomatoes, chopped
1 small aubergine (eggplant), finely chopped
2 courgettes (zucchini), finely chopped
1 red pepper, seeded and finely chopped
salt and pepper

8 tomatoes
100 g / 3 ½ oz / ½ cup black olives, stoned
2 sprigs of basil

Red Peppers with Ratatouille

125

Substitute the tomatoes with 2 red bell peppers.

126

SERVES 4

Breaded Calzone Escalopes

PREPARATION TIME: 10 MINUTES

COOKING TIME: 10 MINUTES

INGREDIENTS

4 slices rose veal escalope
1 ball mozzarella
4 slices Parma ham
4 sage leaves
2 slices white bread, made into breadcrumbs
2 tbsp plain (all purpose) flour
1 egg, beaten
2 tbsp olive oil

- Place the veal between 2 slices film (plastic wrap) and bat out with a rolling pin until very thin.
- Lay a slice of mozzarella and a slice of Parma ham on top of the escalope and lightly press a sage leaf into the ham.
- Roll up the escalope and secure with a toothpick. Repeat for all the escalopes.
- Place the breadcrumbs, flour and egg on separate plates. Dunk the escalopes into the flour, then the egg then the breadcrumbs, coating on all sides.
- Heat the oil in a pan and when hot, add the escalopes and cook on all sides until golden brown and cooked through – approximately 10-12 minutes.
- Serve hot with a salad.

Breaded Calzone with Fontina.

127

Try substituting Fontina for the mozzarella

128

SERVES 4

Italian Cheese and Rocket Soufflé

PREPARATION TIME 10 MINS

COOKING TIME 45 MINS

INGREDIENTS

30g / 1 oz / 1/5 cup butter
2 tbsp plain (all purpose) flour
150ml / 5 fl oz / 2/3 cup milk
60g / 2 oz / 1/5 cup Caciocavallo cheese (or Gruyere or Cheddar), grated
Pinch cayenne pepper
Nutmeg, grated to taste
100g / 3 ½ oz / ½ cup rocket (arugula) leaves, finely chopped
2 large eggs, separated
2 egg whites
1 tbsp Parmesan, grated

- Preheat the oven to 200°C (180° fan) / 400F / gas 6.
- Melt the butter in a pan and stir in the flour. When smooth gradually add the milk, whisking after each addition to make a smooth sauce.
- Once all the milk has been added, stir in the cheese over a low heat, then season and add the cayenne, a little grated nutmeg and stir in the rocket (arugula).
- Mix the 2 egg yolks into the cheese mixture.
- Whisk the 4 egg whites in a large clean mixing bowl to stiff peaks. Fold 1 tbsp of the whites into the cheese mixture to loosen, then, using a metal spoon, carefully fold in the rest in a figure of eight motion to keep the air.
- Spoon the mixture into a greased soufflé dish, or 4 individual ones and sprinkle with Parmesan.
- Place in a roasting in and fill with about 5cm / 2" of boiling water. Place in the oven and bake for 30 minutes. Don't open the door.
- When cooked the soufflé should be risen and golden. Individual soufflés may take a little less cooking time. Serve immediately.

129

SERVES 4

Polenta with Calamari

Polenta with Prawns

130

Substitute the squid for 250g raw prawns, shelled, and proceed as for the squid

Polenta with Stock

131

Substitute the water for chicken stock or vegetable stock instead.

Polenta with Tomatoes

132

Add 2 tbsb of chopped, dried tomatoes and cook the same.

PREPARATION TIME: 50 MINUTES

COOKING TIME: 50 MINUTES

....

INGREDIENTS

225g / 9 oz / 1 cup polenta
1.7 L / 3 pints / 6 cups water
2 tbsp olive oil
1 squid, cleaned and ink sac removed and patted dry
2 tomatoes, finely chopped
2 tbsp black olives, stoned and chopped
1 red chilli, finely chopped
½ lemon, juiced
1 tbsp flat leaf parsley, chopped

- Whisk the polenta slowly into a large pan of boiling salted water.
- As soon as it begins to boil turn the heat down to minimum.
- Stir every 5 minutes or so very thoroughly, ensuring you push the spoon down into the sides of the pan.
- Cook for about 45 minutes until it begins to have the consistency of mashed potato. Season generously with salt and black pepper.
- Oil a tray and tip the polenta out onto to it. Spread the polenta to about 2.5cm / 1" thick. Leave the polenta to cool for about 30 minutes and then cut circles out 5cm / 2" in diameter.
- Meanwhile heat the oil in a pan until nearly smoking.
- Cut the squid across into rings and cut the tentacles into smaller pieces. Add to the pan and fry briskly for about 2 minutes, or until opaque.
- Working quickly, add the tomatoes, olives, chilli and lemon juice and season generously.
- Toss with parsley and remove from the heat.
- Place the polenta circles on a plate, then top with the squid.

133

SERVES 6

Pesto Panna Cotta

Pesto Panna Cotta with Tomatoes

134

Add 1 tbsp sun blushed tomatoes, whizzed to a smooth paste, with the pesto to the cream.

Pesto Panna Cotta with Parma Ham

135

Substitute the cured ham for 6 slices of Parma ham.

Pesto Panna Cotta with Rocket

136

Decorate the finished Panna Cotta with fresh rocket leaves instead of basil.

PREPARATION TIME: 20 MINUTES

COOKING TIME: 5 MINUTES

....

INGREDIENTS

3 leaves of gelatine
500ml / 17 fl oz / 2 cups double (heavy) cream
8 cloves garlic, chopped
4 tbsp basil
1 tbsp pine nuts
Olive oil
1 tomato
6 thin slices of cured ham

- Place the gelatine leaves in cold water.
- Add the garlic and most of the basil leaves to a pestle and mortar and crush with a little olive oil to make a paste.
- Pour 400ml of the cream into a mixer, season and add the pesto. Whisk for a few seconds to amalgamate then pour into a pan.
- Place over a medium heat and bring gently to the boil. When the creams starts to bubble, reduce the heat. Squeeze out the gelatine leaves and add to the cream, whisk and leave to cool a little.
- Whisk the remaining cream to soft peaks. Spoon into the pesto cream, then pour into greased moulds and chill for about 2 hours.
- Before serving, finely dice the tomato or cut into thin rounds. Decorate the pannacotta with ham, tomato and reserved basil leaves.

137

SERVES 4

Black Olive Tapenade

- There are two ways to make tapenade. You can either finely chop all the ingredients for a rougher texture and then stir with olive oil and lemon to amalgamate. Season, being careful with the salt.
- Or you can whiz the ingredients in a food processor for a finer texture, drizzling in the oil and lemon until smooth.
- Serve hot or cold with breadsticks.

PREPARATION TIME:
5-10 MINUTES

INGREDIENTS

250 g / 9 oz / 1 cup black olives, stoned
1 clove of garlic, peeled
100 g / 3 ½ oz / ½ cup sun-dried tomatoes
3 tsp capers
6 anchovies
½ bunch flat leaf parsley
juice of 1 lemon
olive oil
salt and pepper

Green Olive Tapenade

138

Substitute the black olives for green olives and spoon the mixture onto toasted ciabatta bread.

139

SERVES 4

Artichoke Antipasti

- Remove around 4-5 of the toughest outer leaves. Snap away the stem. Spread the leaves apart until you come to the central thinner, lighter leaves. Pull this cone out in one piece and underneath will be the hairy choke; scrape out with a teaspoon.
- Rinse the artichokes with water and place in a bowl of water with lemon juice to prevent discolouring.
- To cook the artichokes, bring salted water to the boil with some lemon juice and cook, uncovered for about 30 minutes or until a leaf pulls away easily and the bases are tender when tested with a skewer.
- Whisk together the first 5 ingredients to a smooth paste and then gradually stir in the olive oil until you have a smooth emulsion.
- To eat the artichokes, serve at room temperature, tearing off a leaf at a time, dipping it into vinaigrette and eating the tender base, discarding the rest of the leaf. Eat the heart in the middle too.

PREPARATION TIME 10 MINS

COOKING TIME 45 MINS

INGREDIENTS

4 globe artichokes
lemon juice

FOR THE VINAIGRETTE:

1 tsp salt
1 clove of garlic, crushed
1 tsp Dijon mustard
1 tbsp balsamic vinegar
black pepper
6 tbsp extra virgin olive oil

Spicy Artichokes

140

Add ½ tsp of chilli flakes to the mixture for a spicy kick.

141

MAKES 8

Seafood Pizzas

PREPARATION TIME:

45 MINUTES + PROVING TIME

COOKING TIME: 8-10 MINUTES

INGREDIENTS

FOR THE PIZZA DOUGH:
400 g / 13 ½ oz / 1 ½ cups strong white bread flour
100 g / 3 ½ oz / ½ cup fine ground semolina flour
½ tbsp salt
1 x 7 g sachet dried yeast
½ tbsp caster (superfine) sugar
Approx 350 ml / ½ pint / ⅓ cup lukewarm water

FOR THE TOPPING:
10 tbsp bottled passata
200 g / 6 ½ oz / ¾ cup raw prawns, shelled
1 scallop per pizza
handful black olives, stoned
1 green chilli, finely sliced
basil, to garnish

- Pour the flours and salt into a bowl and make a well in the centre. Add the yeast and sugar to the water and mix. When frothing, pour into the well.
- Slowly bring in the flour from around the insides and mix into the water. When it starts coming together, pat it into a ball. Knead for 10 minutes until smooth.
- Flour the dough, cover with film and leave to rest for 30 minutes.
- Preheat the oven to 250ºC (230 º fan) / 500F / gas 9. Flour the surface, tear off a piece of dough and roll into a circle about 0.5 cm thick.
- Dust each one with flour and lay out on the surface.
- Spread 1 tbsp of passata on each pizza, and then top each one with the olives, prawns and chilli.
- Slice the scallops in half and place into the prawns. Place on a preheated baking sheet for 10 minutes until golden.

Mussel and Shrimp Pizza

 142

Replace the prawns and scallops with mussels and shrimps.

143

SERVES 6-8

Mini Tomato Anchovy Tarts

PREPARATION TIME: 30 MINUTES

COOKING TIME: 12 MINUTES

INGREDIENTS

1 pack ready-rolled puff pastry
1 tbsp butter
1 onion, peeled and finely chopped
2 cloves of garlic, finely chopped
200ml / 6 ½ fl oz / ¾ cup passata
small handful oregano leaves
salt and pepper
1-2 ripe tomatoes, thickly sliced
8 black olives, stoned and halved
8 anchovy fillets

- Preheat the oven to 200°C (180° fan) / 400F / gas 6.
- Cut out pastry circles about 7cm in diameter from the sheet. You should make between 6 and 8.
- Place on a greased baking sheet and bake in the oven for 12 minutes until crisp and golden.
- When cooked, push the middle of each pastry circle down a little with a spoon to create a space for the filling.
- Heat the butter in a pan and cook the onion and garlic until golden.
- Add the passata and oregano and heat briskly until reduced and thick. Adjust the seasoning..
- Spoon into the middle of the pastry cases, then top with a slice of fresh tomato.
- Place the anchovy and 2 olive halves on top and grill until bubbling.
- Leave to cool before eating.

Mini Tomato and Cheese Tarts **144**

Swap the anchovies for cheese to make a vegetarian option.

145

SERVES 4

Minestrone

Light Minestrone
146

Omit the tomatoes for a fresher-flavoured soup.

Green Minestrone
147

Use finely diced courgettes and green beans, adding them in with the pasta.

Minestrone with Olives
148

Add 100 g / 3 ½ oz / ½ cup black pitted and chopped olives with the greens and cook the same.

PREPARATION TIME: 20 MINUTES

COOKING TIME: 1 ½ HOURS

INGREDIENTS

2 tbsp olive oil
50 g / 1 ½ oz / 1/5 cup pancetta
1 onion, peeled and finely chopped
2 celery stalks, finely chopped
2 carrots, peeled and finely chopped
2 cloves of garlic, finely chopped
2 potatoes, peeled and finely chopped
2 tomatoes, peeled and finely chopped
1.5 L / 2 ½ pints / 5 ½ cups chicken stock
200 g / 6 ½ oz / ¾ cup greens, finely sliced
100 g / 3 ½ oz / ½ cup macaroni pasta
salt and pepper
Parmesan cheese
extra virgin olive oil

- Heat the oil in a large pan and fry off the pancetta until the fat runs and it starts to turn golden.
- Add the vegetables in the order above, giving each one a good 5 minutes to cook without colouring, stirring regularly, before adding the next one.
- Pour in the stock and bring to a gentle simmer, then cook very gently for about an hour.
- Add the greens and the pasta and cook for a further 30 minutes.
- Adjust the seasoning.
- Serve warm, sprinkled with Parmesan and drizzled with olive oil.

Italian Vegetable Tart

PREPARATION TIME: 40 MINUTES

COOKING TIME: 35-40 MINUTES

INGREDIENTS

FOR THE TART
2 x 375 g packs ready-rolled
shortcrust pastry
1 egg, beaten

FOR THE FILLING
olive oil
1 onion, peeled and finely chopped
2 cloves of garlic, finely sliced
1 aubergine (eggplant), cut into thin
slices
2 courgettes (zucchini), cut into thin
slices
1 jar roasted red peppers
2 eggs, beaten
275 ml / 10 fl oz / 1 cup double
(heavy) cream
salt and pepper

- Preheat the oven to 180°C (160° fan) / 350F / gas 4.
- Roll out 1 pastry sheet and use to line a pie dish.
- Heat the oil in a pan and cook the onion and garlic until golden. Move from the pan to a bowl using a slotted spoon.
- Add the aubergine (eggplant) and a drop of oil and cook until tender, taking care to try to keep the slices intact. Place them on kitchen paper and repeat with the courgette slices.
- Layer the vegetables with the peppers in the base of the pie dish, alternating the layers.
- Whisk together the eggs and cream, season and pour over the vegetables.
- Roll out the remaining pastry sheet and cut into 1 cm wide strips. Use them to form a lattice on top of the pie.
- Bake in the oven for around 35-40 minutes until the pastry is golden. Serve warm.

Chicken and Cheese Pizzas

PREPARATION TIME:
45 MINUTES + PROVING TIME

COOKING TIME: 8-10 MINUTES

INGREDIENTS

FOR THE PIZZA DOUGH:
400 g / 13 ½ oz / 1 ½ cups strong
white bread flour
100 g / 3 ½ oz / ½ cup fine ground
semolina flour
½ tbsp salt
1 x 7 g sachet dried yeast
½ tbsp caster (superfine) sugar
350 ml / ½ pint / ⅓ cup lukewarm
water

FOR THE TOPPING:
1 onion, sliced
2 tbsp butter
2 chicken breasts, skinned and
chopped
80 g / 3 oz / ⅓ cup Fourme d'Ambert
cheese per pizza

- Pour the flour and salt into a bowl and make a well.
- Add the yeast and sugar to the water and mix. When frothing, pour into the well.
- Bring in the flour from around the insides and mix into the water. When it starts to come together, pat it into a ball. Knead for 10 minutes, then flour the dough, cover with film and leave to rest for 30 minutes.
- Cook the onion and butter in a pan until golden.
- Add the chicken and cook until the chicken is golden and tender.
- Roll the pizzas out about 30 minutes before you want to cook them. Preheat the oven to 250°C (230° fan) / 500F / gas 9. Flour the surface, tear off a piece of dough and roll into a circle about 0.5cm thick.
- Dust each one with flour and lay out on the surface.
- Top with the chicken, onions and sliced cheese. Place on a preheated baking sheet for 8-10 minutes until golden.

Chicken and Tomato Pizza

151

Omit the chicken and substitute sliced
tomatoes or even cooked sliced new potatoes.

152

SERVES 3-4

Pizza Four Seasons

- Pour the flours and salt into a bowl and make a well in the centre. Add the yeast and sugar, mix and leave for a few minutes. Once frothing, pour into the well.
- Using a fork in a circular movement, slowly mix the flour into the water. When it starts coming together, use your hands to pat it into a ball.
- Knead for 10 minutes, until it is smooth and elastic.
- Flour and cover with film. Leave to rest for 30 minutes.
- Roll the pizzas out 30 minutes before cooking.
- Preheat the oven to 250°C (230° fan) / 500F / gas 9. Flour the surface, tear off a piece of dough and roll into a circle. Dust each circle with a little flour.
- Spread the base of each with passata, then top each quarter with one of the ingredients and sprinkle the mozzarella cheese all over.
- Place on a preheated baking sheet for 8-10 minutes until golden and crisp.

PREPARATION TIME: 45 MINUTES + PROVING TIME

COOKING TIME: 8-10 MINUTES

INGREDIENTS

For the dough:
400 g / 13 ½ oz / 1 ½ cups strong white bread flour
100 g / 3 ½ oz / ½ cup fine ground semolina flour
½ tbsp salt
1 x 7 g sachet dried yeast
½ tbsp caster (superfine) sugar
350 ml / ½ pint / 1 ½ cups lukewarm water
For the topping, per pizza:
6 tbsp bottled passata
2 slices ham
3 button mushrooms, thinly sliced
6 black olives, stoned
4 artichoke hearts, halved
80 g / 3 oz / ¼ cup mozzarella
extra virgin olive oil

Pizza with Parma Ham

153

Add 100 g / 3 oz / ½ cup Parma ham to the top of the pizzas before cooking.

154

SERVES 2

Mozzarella Fritters

- Mix the bread with salt and pepper and the chilli flakes in a food processor to make breadcrumbs.
- Slice the mozzarella into ½ cm slices
- Tip the flour onto one plate and the eggs into another.
- Coat the mozzarella slices in the breadcrumbs
- Dunk the crumbed slices into the egg, then the flour, then the egg again.
- Heat about 1cm / 1/2" depth of oil in a pan until a cube of bread sizzles when dunked in.
- Fry the crumbed mozzarella in the oil, turning carefully, until golden and crisp on all sides.
- Drain on kitchen paper and serve hot.

PREPARATION TIME: 10 MINUTES

COOKING TIME: 10-15 MINUTES

INGREDIENTS

6 slices white bread, crusts removed
Salt and pepper
Pinch dried chilli flakes
1 ball mozzarella
3 heaped tbsp plain (all purpose) flour
2 eggs, beaten
Vegetable oil, for frying

Ricotta Fritters

155

Replace the mozzarella for 450g / 14 oz / 2 cups of ricotta and cook the same.

156
SERVES 4

Creamed Yellow Pepper Soup

Red Pepper and Tomato Soup

157

Use 4 red peppers and 2 finely chopped tomatoes in place of the yellow peppers.

Green Pepper Soup

158

Use 4 green peppers in place of the yellow peppers.

PREPARATION TIME: 5 MINUTES

COOKING TIME: 40 MINUTES

INGREDIENTS

1 ciabatta loaf
olive oil
25 g / 1 oz butter
1 onion, finely chopped
1 clove of garlic, finely chopped
4 yellow peppers, finely chopped
750 ml / 1 ¼ pints / 3 cups chicken stock
120 ml / 4 fl oz / ½ cup double (heavy) cream
salt and pepper

- Preheat the oven to 180°C / 350F / gas 5. Tear the ciabatta into large croutons and toss with olive oil. Place on a baking sheet.
- Bake in the oven for 10-12 minutes, until golden and crunchy and then set aside on kitchen paper.
- Heat the butter in a pan, then sweat the onion and garlic without colouring.
- Add the peppers and cook for a further 10 minutes until they have softened.
- Pour over the stock and simmer for 25 minutes, until the peppers are completely tender.
- Allow to cool slightly and then whiz in a liquidiser until smooth.
- Transfer back to the pan and stir in the cream, heating gently.
- Adjust the seasoning before serving.

159

MAKES 40

Tomato and Basil Crostini

- Preheat the oven to 200°C (180° fan) / 400F / gas 7. Place the cherry tomatoes in a roasting tin and drizzle with oil, salt and pepper. Sprinkle over the herbs and roast in the oven for about 25 minutes or until lightly charred and wizened.
- Slice the ficelle into rounds about 1cm / ½ " thick.
- Dab each one with a little oil and bake in the oven until lightly golden and crisp , for about 8 minutes.
- Rub the crostini with the garlic. Push the tomatoes to one side in the tin and lightly press each crostini into the roasting juices to soak into the bread a little.
- Top each crostini with a cherry tomato and sprinkle over the basil.

PREPARATION TIME: 10 MINUTES

COOKING TIME: 25 MINUTES

INGREDIENTS

1 ficelle
olive oil
40 cherry tomatoes
2 sprigs rosemary leaves, finely chopped
2 cloves of garlic, halved
bunch basil leaves
extra virgin olive oil

Mushroom and Basil Crostini

160

Replace the tomato for 450g / 14 oz / 2 cups chopped mushrooms, and sauté for 5 minutes.

161

MAKES 6-8

Bruschetta

- Preheat the oven and bake the ciabatta loaf according to packet instructions. Once cooked, leave to cool.
- When cool, cut the loaf into 1.5 cm thick slices.
- Meanwhile slice the tomatoes and sprinkle with a little salt.
- Heat a griddle pan until very hot and lay the bread on the griddle. If you don't have a griddle you can do this under the grill until the bread is lightly toasted.
- Rub the toasted side with the cut garlic and drizzle with olive oil.
- Slice the mozzarella and lay with the tomatoes on the toasted bread and scatter with chopped olives.
- Scatter over the basil before serving.

PREPARATION TIME: 15 MINUTES

COOKING TIME: 8 MINUTES

INGREDIENTS

1 ciabatta loaf
extra virgin olive oil
2 cloves of garlic, halved
300 g / 10 oz / 1 ¼ cups mozzarella
5 very ripe vine-grown tomatoes, room temperature
black olives, chopped
salt and pepper
basil

Bruschetta with Pesto

162

Spread a little pesto on the bruschetta before the toppings.

163

SERVES 4

Seafood Minestrone

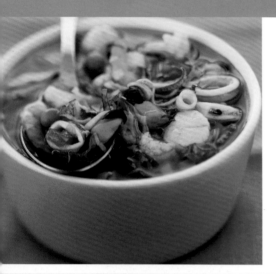

PREPARATION TIME: 10 MINUTES

COOKING TIME: 35-40 MINUTES

INGREDIENTS

1 tbsp olive oil
1 onion, peeled and finely chopped
1 carrot, peeled and finely chopped
1 celery stalk, peeled and chopped
2 tomatoes, finely chopped
1 L / 2 pints / 4 ¼ cups chicken stock
50 g / 1 ½ oz / ⅕ cup macaroni pasta
750 g / 1 ¼ lb / 3 cups mixed raw seafood, such as prawns, scallops, mussels and squid
1 bunch parsley, chopped
½ lemon
salt and pepper

- Heat the olive oil in a pan and sweat the onion, carrot and celery without colouring for 5 minutes.
- Add the tomatoes and cook for a further 2 minutes.
- Pour over the stock, bring to a simmer and add the pasta.
- Cook for about 20 minutes until the pasta is tender.
- Add the seafood and poach in the soup until the prawns turn pink, the scallops opaque and the mussels open. Discard any that remain closed.
- Scatter over the parsley and adjust the seasoning.

164

SERVES 6-8

Crostini with Bayonne Ham

PREPARATION TIME:
45 MINUTES + 3 HOURS

COOKING TIME: 10
MINUTES

INGREDIENTS

4-5 ripe vine-grown plum tomatoes
1 ciabatta loaf, ready-to-bake

extra virgin olive oil
2 cloves of garlic, halved
300 g / 10 oz / 1 ¼ cups mozzarella
8 slices Bayonne ham
salt and pepper
basil

- Preheat the oven to 100°C (80° fan) / 200F / gas 1. Slice the tomatoes in half and scoop out the seeds. Salt the insides and leave to drain.
- Place in a roasting tin, drizzle with a little oil and bake for 3 hours. Remove from the oven and set aside.
- Heat the oven and bake the ciabatta loaf according to packet instructions. Leave to cool and firm up.
- When cool, cut the loaf into 1.5 cm thick slices. Meanwhile slice the tomatoes and sprinkle with a little salt.
- Heat a griddle pan and lay the bread on the griddle until you achieve char marks across both sides. If you don't have a griddle you can do this under the grill until the bread is lightly toasted.
- Rub the toasted side with the cut garlic and drizzle with olive oil.
- Lay half a slice of ham on each piece, then top with a little mozzarella.
- Place a tomato half on top. Garnish with basil.

Crostini with Parma Ham

165

Replace the same amount of Bayonne ham with Parma ham.

166

MAKES 40

Crostini with Coppa

- Preheat the oven to 180°C (160° fan) / 350F / gas 5. Slice the ficelle into rounds, about 1cm thick.
- Dab each one with a little oil and bake in the oven until lightly golden and crisp , for about 8 minutes.
- Slice the Coppa ham and tomatoes in half. Slice the cheese into small pieces.
- Wrap a tomato half, a piece of cheese and a basil leaf in the ham and place on top of the the crostini.

PREPARATION TIME:
25-30 MINUTES

COOKING TIME: 8 MINUTES

INGREDIENTS

1 ficelle
olive oil
20 slices Coppa ham
20 sun-blush tomatoes
100g / 3 1/2 oz / ½ cup Emmental cheese
½ bunch basil leaves

Crostini with Artichoke and Olives

167

Replace the Coppa ham and tomatoes for 400 g / 14 oz / 1 ½ cups artichoke hearts and 1 tbsp pitted olives.

168

MAKES 40

Mushroom Crostini

- Preheat the oven to 180°C (160° fan) / 350F / gas 5. Slice the ficelle into rounds about 1cm thick.
- Dab each one with a little oil and bake in the oven until lightly golden and crisp , for about 8 minutes.
- Whiz the mushrooms and onion in a food processor until finely chopped.
- Heat the butter in a pan and cook the mushrooms and onions with the garlic for about 25-30 minutes until all the water has evaporated.
- Season and stir in enough cream just to bind.
- Top the crostini with the mushroom mixture.

PREPARATION TIME:
30-40 MINUTES

COOKING TIME: 8 MINUTES

INGREDIENTS

1 ficelle
olive oil
250g / 9 oz / 1 cup mushrooms
1 onion, peeled
2 tbsp butter
2 cloves of garlic, very finely chopped
nutmeg
salt and pepper
juice of ½ lemon
2 tbsp double cream, to bind

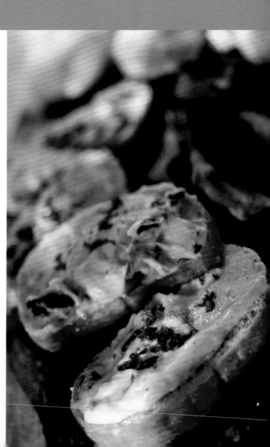

Mushroom and Thyme Crostini

169

Add 2 sprigs of thyme into the mixture with the cream.

170

MAKES 18

Farfalle Primavera

PREPARATION TIME: 5 MINUTES

COOKING TIME: 15 MINUTES

INGREDIENTS

70 g / 2 ½ oz / ⅕ cup farfalle pasta
per person
olive oil
½ bunch asparagus, trimmed
100 g / 3 ½ oz / ½ cup peas, fresh
or frozen
100 g / 3 ½ oz / ½ cup broad beans,
double-podded
50g / 1 ½ oz / 1/5 cup butter
2 tsp Parmesan, grated
lemon juice
salt and pepper

- Cook the pasta in boiling salted water according to packet instructions. Drain, reserving a little of the cooking water, then toss with little olive oil to prevent sticking.
- Meanwhile steam the asparagus until nearly tender – check after 4 minutes, then keep checking.
- Briefly cook the peas and beans for 2-3 minutes until just tender.
- Heat the butter in a pan and add the vegetables. Cook for 1 minute then add the pasta and reserved water.
- Toss together and then sprinkle over the Parmesan.
- Adjust the seasoning and serve.

Linguine Primavera

171

Substitute the Farfalle for 70 g / 2 ½ oz / ¼ cup of Linguine and cook the same.

172

SERVES 4

Minestrone and Squash

PREPARATION TIME: 30 MINUTES

COOKING TIME: 2 HOURS

INGREDIENTS

2 tbsp olive oil
50g / 1 ½ oz / ⅕ cup pancetta or
smoked streaky bacon
1 onion, peeled and finely chopped
2 celery stalks, finely chopped
2 carrots, peeled and finely chopped
2 cloves of garlic, finely chopped
2 potatoes, peeled and finely
chopped
2 tomatoes, peeled and finely
chopped
1.5 l / 2 ½ pints / 5 cups chicken stock
200 g / 6 ½ oz / ¾ cup greens, such as
cavolo nero or savoy cabbage, finely
sliced
100 g / 3 ½ oz / ½ cup macaroni pasta
salt and pepper

- Preheat the oven to 200ºC (180 º fan) / 400F / gas 7. Cut the top off each squash and use a spoon to hollow out the insides.
- Sprinkle with a little salt and leave to drain upside down on kitchen towel for 30 minutes.
- Meanwhile, heat the oil in a large pan and fry off the pancetta until the fat runs and it starts to turn golden.
- Add the vegetables in the order given, giving each one 5 minutes to cook without colouring, stirring regularly, before adding the next one.
- Pour in the stock and bring to a gently simmer, then cook for an hour. Pat the squash dry then roast in the oven with a little olive oil for 30 minutes.
- Add the greens and the pasta to the soup and cook for a further 30 minutes. Remove the cooked squash from the oven and keep warm.
- When the soup is ready to serve, ladle into the squash.

Minestrone with Young Spinach

173

Substitute the greens for young spinach and cook the same.

174

SERVES 4

Antipasti

- Preheat a grill to very hot or open up a gas flame to full.
- Roast the peppers under the grill or over the flame until completely blackened and blistered all over.
- Place the peppers in a plastic bag and seal and set aside.
- Repeat the process with the aubergine (eggplant). Alternatively you could roast the aubergine (eggplant) whole in a very hot oven until blackened and collapsed – about 1 hour.
- Slice the aubergine (eggplant) in half and scoop out the middle into a bowl. Discard the skin.
- Dress the aubergine (eggplant) with olive oil and balsamic vinegar and season. Peel the skin off the peppers. It should come away easily, but try to keep the flesh whole.
- Lay the roasted pepper flat on a serving platter along with any juices from the bag.
- Spoon the aubergine (eggplant) around and scatter over pine nuts and Parmesan before serving at room temperature.

PREPARATION TIME:
30-60 MINUTES

INGREDIENTS

4 red peppers
1 aubergine (eggplant)
2-3 tbsp extra virgin olive oil
1 tbsp balsamic vinegar
salt and pepper
1 tbsp pine nuts, lightly toasted
Parmesan shavings

Antipasti with Peppers

 175

Use 2 yellow peppers and 2 red peppers for a really eye-popping plate

176

SERVES 4

Grilled Polenta with Antipasti

- Whisk the polenta slowly in a pan of boiling water. As soon as it begins to boil cover with a lid slightly askew and turn the heat down.
- When it begins to thicken, stir every 5 minutes. Cook for 45 minutes until it develops the consistency of mashed potato and season generously.
- Oil a tray and tip the polenta out onto to it. Spread the polenta 2.5 cm thick. Leave it to cool for 30 minutes and then cut into squares.
- Preheat the oven to 200°C (180° fan) / 400F / gas 7.
- Cut the 'cheeks' off the peppers and roast in the oven with a little oil and seasoning until tender. Place in a plastic bag and leave for 20 minutes.
- Peel the skins off the peppers when cool.
- Cut the topping ingredients into bite-size pieces and use to top the polenta squares before serving.

PREPARATION TIME:
20 MINUTES + COOLING TIME

COOKING TIME: 45-60 MINUTES

INGREDIENTS

225 g / 9 oz / 1 cup polenta
1.7 l / 3 pints / 6 cups water
2 red peppers
olive oil
salt and pepper
2 handfuls, black olives, stoned
4 slices Parma ham
jar of artichoke hearts
Parmesan

Grilled Parmesan Polenta

 177

Use 100 g of grated Parmesan in the polenta towards the end of cooking.

178

SERVES 6

Pumpkin Gnocchi

Pumpkin and Ricotta Gnocchi

179

Add 200 g / 7 oz / ¾ cup ricotta and cook the same.

Butternut Squash Gnocchi

180

Omit the pumpkin for ½ a de-seeded and diced butternut squash, roast in the oven with a sprig of thyme for 20 minutes.

Gnocchi with Spinach

181

Replace the pumpkin with 400 g / 13 ½ oz / 1 ½ cups spinach, wilted over a high heat and squeezed completely dry of excess moisture.

PREPARATION TIME: 10 MINUTES

COOKING TIME: 50 MINUTES

INGREDIENTS

400 g / 13 ½ oz / 1 ½ cups pumpkin, peeled
250 g / 9 oz / 1 cup potatoes, peeled
2 eggs
500 g / 1 lb / 2 cups flour
salt and pepper

- Cut the pumpkin and potato into cubes and steam for 30-45 minutes, until tender.
- Push through a potato ricer to make a smooth puree, or mash thoroughly until there are no lumps.
- Add the eggs, mix well, then add the flour and stir until completely combined. The mixture should be fairly stiff and you should be able to shape it.
- Form into small balls and press down lightly on one side with a fork to give the gnocchi shape.
- Bring a large pan of salted water to the boil and tip in the gnocchi. When they float to the surface they are cooked, so remove with a slotted spoon and leave to drain on kitchen paper.
- Reheat immediately in a pan, with butter and Parmesan or your favourite pasta sauce.

182

SERVES 4

Tomato, Mozzarella and Ham Sala

- Slice the tomatoes thickly, drizzle with oil and a little salt and leave to stand for 10 minutes.
- Tear the mozzarella into pieces.
- Arrange the tomatoes and mozzarella in an alternating pattern on a serving platter, drizzling over the juices from the tomatoes.
- Lay the ham alongside.
- Scatter over torn basil leaves and drizzle with more oil and a little pepper.

PREPARATION TIME: 15 MINUTES

INGREDIENTS

4 ripe vine-grown tomatoes
2 buffalo mozzarella balls
salt and pepper
extra virgin olive oil
8 slices Parma ham
basil

Mozzarella, Ham and Chilli Salad

183

Use a pinch of dried chilli flakes over the mozzarella for a kick.

184

SERVES 4

Melon and Parma Ham

- Cut the melon in half and scoop out and discard the seeds.
- Using a vegetable peeler or a very sharp knife cut away thin slices of melon by running your implement along the cut flesh.
- Place the slices in a small bowl, slightly overlapping to form a well in the centre for the ham.
- Roll the ham slices into rose shapes and place in the centre.
- Drizzle with a little oil and sprinkle the melon with a little salt to bring out the sweetness.

PREPARATION TIME: 15 MINUTES

INGREDIENTS

1 Cantaloupe melon, very ripe
8 slices Parma ham
extra virgin olive oil
sea salt

Melon, Parma Ham and Basil

185

Sprinkle some freshly torn basil leaves on top of the melon.

Italian-Style Vegetables

MAKES 18

PREPARATION TIME: 10 MINUTES

COOKING TIME: 40 MINUTES

INGREDIENTS

1 aubergine (eggplant)
2 courgettes (zucchini)
2 red peppers, deseeded
2 onions, peeled
2 cloves garlic, whole
2 tbsp rosemary leaves, finely chopped
4 tbsp olive oil

- Preheat the oven to 200°C (180° fan) / 400F / gas 6.
- Slice the aubergine (eggplant) and courgettes (zucchini) into thick rounds about 1cm / ½" in width.
- Cut the peppers into large pieces.
- Slice the onion into thick rings.
- Tip the vegetables into a roasting tin and toss with the garlic, rosemary and seasoning and drizzle with oil.
- Roast for about 30-40 minutes until all is tender and golden.

Italian-Style Vegetables with Balsamic
 187

At the end of cooking, drizzle with 2 tbsp balsamic vinegar

 188

SERVES 4

Caponata Stuffed Aubergine

PREPARATION TIME: 20 MINUTES

COOKING TIME: 45 MINUTES

INGREDIENTS

2 aubergines (eggplants)
4 tbsp olive oil
1 tsp dried oregano
1 onion, peeled and finely chopped
2 cloves of garlic, peeled and finely sliced
2 celery stalks, chopped
bunch of flat leaf parsley, chopped
2 tbsp capers, drained
12 green olives, stoned
3 tbsp red wine vinegar
4 ripe tomatoes, chopped
salt and pepper

- Preheat the oven to 200°C (180° fan) / 400F / gas 6.
- Cut the aubergines in half lengthways, drizzle with 2 tbsp oil and bake in the oven for about 30 minutes until tender.
- Remove the flesh with a spoon, leaving the skin intact and with a margin of flesh to support the structure.
- Heat the rest of the olive oil in the pan and cook the onion with oregano, garlic and celery until softened.
- Add the aubergine and the rest of the ingredients and simmer for around 15 minutes until the vinegar has evaporated.
- Season and spoon into the aubergine skins.
- Serve immediately.

Almond Stuffed Aubergines
189

Add 2 tbsp flaked almonds, lightly toasted to the mixture.

190

SERVES 4

Italian Summer Brochettes

- Halve the tomatoes and drizzle with oil and salt and chilli flakes. Leave to macerate for 10 minutes.
- Tear the mozzarella into chunks.
- Thread onto skewers, alternating the tomatoes, cheese and basil leaves.
- Drizzle with the tomato juices.

PREPARATION TIME: 15 MINUTES

COOKING TIME: N/A

INGREDIENTS

300g / 10 oz / 1 ¼ cups cherry tomatoes
2 tbsp olive oil
Pinch salt
Pinch dried chilli flakes
2 balls buffalo mozzarella
1 handful basil leaves

Italian Brochettes with Avocado

191

Thread on chunks of avocado or rolled up slices of cured ham

Italian Brochettes with Pesto

192

Drizzle with green pesto sauce before serving.

193

SERVES 4

Red Pepper Involtini

- Preheat the oven to 200°C (180° fan) / 400 F/ gas 7.
- Seed and core the pepper and then roast whole with a little oil until tender but not too blackened.
- Open out the peppers and cut each one into 2 rectangles and set aside.
- Toast ¾ of the pine nuts in a dry frying pan until lightly golden.
- Add to a food processor with the cream cheese, Parmesan, parsley, zest and a little seasoning and whiz until smooth.
- Stir in the whole pine nuts.
- Spoon the filling down one side of each pepper rectangle, then roll the pepper up to make a roulade.
- Serve at room temperature.

PREPARATION TIME: 10 MINUTES

COOKING TIME: 30 MINUTES

INGREDIENTS

4 red peppers
olive oil
FOR THE FILLING:
100g / 3 ½ oz / ½ cup pine nuts
100g / 3 ½ oz / ½ cup cream cheese
1 tbsp Parmesan, grated
½ bunch flat leaf parsley
zest of 1 lemon
salt and pepper

Yellow Pepper Involtini

194

Try yellow peppers instead of red for a fruitier taste.

195

SERVES 2

Italian Bread

Fennel Bread

196

Add a teaspoon of fennel seeds in place of the rosemary.

Onion Bread

197

Works great with half a finely sliced onion mixed in with the rosemary.

Chilli Bread

198

Substitute the rosemary with chilli flakes for a spicy kick.

PREPARATION TIME: 10 MINUTES

COOKING TIME: 25 MINUTES

INGREDIENTS

450ml / 1 pint / 2 cups water
210g / 7 oz / ¾ cup chickpea (gram) flour
3 tbsp olive oil
½ tsp salt
1 tsp rosemary leaves, finely chopped

- Mix the water with the chickpea (gram) flour, 1 tbsp oil and the salt in a large bowl.
- Cover and leave to rest for 2 hours.
- Preheat the oven to 200°C (180° fan) / 400F / gas 6..
- Heat a large oven-proof frying pan with the remaining oil.
- Skim off any foam from the batter and stir in the rosemary.
- Pour the batter into the pan and place in the oven for 25 minutes until brown and crisp.
- Sprinkle with sea salt before serving.

199

SERVES 4

Tomato Olive and Pine Nut Pizza

- Flour the dough, cover with film (plastic wrap) and leave to rest for 30 minutes.
- Roll the pizzas out about 30 minutes before you want to cook them. Preheat the oven to 200°C (180° fan) / 400F / gas 6. Flour the surface, tear off a piece of dough and roll into a rough circle about 1cm / ½" thick.
- Dust each one with a little flour and lay out on the surface.
- Spread the base of each pizza with passata. Top with the tomatoes, olives, pine nuts and mozzarella.
- Place either directly on the bars of the oven or on a preheated baking sheet for 8-10 minutes until golden and crisp.
- Drizzle with extra virgin olive oil, grind over some pepper, scatter over the basil and serve hot.

PREPARATION TIME:
1 HOUR 30 MINUTES

COOKING TIME: 8-10 MINUTES

INGREDIENTS

500g / 1lb pizza dough

FOR THE TOPPING
(Per pizza)
6 tbsp passata
100g / 3 ½ oz / ½ cup red and yellow cherry tomatoes, halved
Handful black olives, stoned
1 tbsp pine nuts, lightly toasted
½ ball mozzarella, sliced
Handful basil leaves
1 tbsp olive oil

Goat's cheese pizza

200

Replace the mozzarella with slices of goat's cheese for a creamier texture.

201

MAKES 40

Florentine Crostini

- Preheat the oven to 180°C (160° fan) / 350F / gas 5. Slice the ficelle into rounds about 1cm, thick.
- Dab each one with a little oil and bake in the oven until lightly golden and crisp , for about 8 minutes.
- Process the celery, garlic, shallot, lemon zest, anchovies and parsley in a food processor until very finely chopped.
- Heat the oil in a pan and cook gently for about 5 minutes until softened.
- Drain the chicken livers, dry and chop them fairly small, then add to the pan and cook, stirring regularly for about 5-7 minutes or until still pink inside but golden outside.
- Add the wine and allow to bubble up and reduce down to a syrup.
- Season and add the capers. Remove from the heat and leave to cool a little before spreading onto the crostini.

PREPARATION TIME: 20 MINUTES

COOKING TIME: 20 MINUTES

INGREDIENTS

1 ficelle
olive oil
400g / 13 ½ oz / 1 ½ cups chicken livers, cleaned and soaked in a little milk
1 celery stalk
1 clove of garlic, peeled
2 shallots, peeled
bunch flat leaf parsley
zest of ¼ lemon
3 anchovy fillets, chopped
2 tbsp olive oil
6 tbsp white wine
salt and pepper
2 tsp capers, drained and chopped

Florentine Sultana Crostini

202

Add a handful of golden sultanas to the crostini topping, along with the wine.

MAIN DISHES

Macaroni with Beef Stew

203
SERVES 6

PREPARATION TIME: 45 MINUTES
+ OVERNIGHT MARINATING

COOKING TIME:
3 HOURS 30 MINUTES

INGREDIENTS

2 carrots, peeled and chopped
1 onion, peeled and chopped
1 onion, whole
1 cloves garlic, peeled
2 cloves garlic, peeled and chopped
1 bouquet garni
600 g / 1 lb 5 oz / 4 cups stewing beef, cubed
3 tbsp olive oil
2 cloves
125 g / 4 ½ oz / ¾ cup smoked bacon lardons
1 tbsp tomato puree
550 ml / 1 pint / 2 cups beef stock
500 g / 1 lb 2 oz / 4 ½ cups macaroni pasta

- Combine the carrots, ½ onion and 1 garlic clove in a food processor. Peel the remaining onion, cut in half and push the cloves into it.
- Place in a large bowl with the bouquet garni and the meat. Season and add 1 tbsp of oil and cover with film and leave to marinade overnight.
- Remove the meat from the marinade, pat dry and fry in batches to seal all sides. Return all the meat plus the marinade to a casserole pan.
- Add the lardons, garlic and onion and fry gently, stir in the tomato puree. Season and cook for 10 minutes.
- Add the stock and turn up the heat until simmering. Cover and cook over a low heat for 3 hours.
- Cook the pasta according to packet instructions. Drain and toss with a little butter to prevent sticking.
- Fish the cloved onion and bouquet garni out of the stew and serve with the pasta.

Macaroni with Pork Stew

 204

Use cubed pork or rose veal instead of beef.

205
SERVES 6

Artichoke and Feta Cannelloni

PREPARATION TIME: 30 MINUTES

COOKING TIME:
1 HOUR 15 MINUTES

INGREDIENTS

6 globe artichokes
1 lemon, juiced
4 tbsp olive oil
1 onion, peeled and chopped
2 cloves garlic, chopped
200 ml / 7 fl. oz / ⅘ cup white wine
12 sheets of lasagna pasta
200 g / 7 oz / 1 ⅓ cups feta
400 ml / 14 fl. oz / 2 cups passata
2 tbsp basil, chopped

- Remove some of the tough outer leaves of the artichokes, snap off the stalk and snap away the stem.
- Spread the leaves apart and dig out the central cone with a teaspoon. Scrape out the choke underneath.
- Place the artichokes in acidulated water. Heat the oil in a casserole pan and add the artichokes, onion, garlic and white wine and cook for 1 hour.
- Meanwhile, preheat the oven to 180°C (160° fan) / 350F / gas 4. Cook the lasagna sheets according to packet instructions. Drain and lay out on a work surface.
- Chop the basil and feta, setting a little aside for the sauce. Spoon the artichoke mixture and feta and basil down one half of each sheet then roll up to form a cylinder.
- Place in a roasting tin and cover with tomato sauce and sprinkle with reserved feta and basil. Bake for 15 minutes and serve warm.

Artichoke and Taleggio Cannelloni

206

Use a melting cheese such as Taleggio instead of feta.

207

SERVES 4

Tagliatelle Carbonara

- Cook the pasta in boiling salted water according to packet instructions.
- Heat the butter in a pan and fry the pancetta until golden.
- Whisk the egg yolks and Parmesan into the cream.
- Drain the pasta, return to the pan and, working quickly, scrape the pancetta and butter into the pan and toss.
- Toss off the heat with the egg / cream mixture then serve immediately.

PREPARATION TIME: 5 MINUTES

COOKING TIME: 12 MINUTES

INGREDIENTS

500 g / 1 lb 2 oz/ 2 cups tagliatelle
2 tbsp butter
12 slices pancetta, chopped
4 egg yolks
100 ml / 3 ½ fl. oz / ½ cup double (heavy) cream
2 tbsp Parmesan, grated

Tagliatelle Carbonara with Peas

208

Replace the pancetta with 200 g / 7 oz cooked peas.

209

SERVES 4

Spaghetti in Tomato Sauce

- Cook the pasta in salted boiling water according to packet instructions. Drain and toss with a little extra virgin olive oil and keep warm.
- Heat the oil in a pan with the garlic for a few minutes.
- When the garlic starts to sizzle, increase the heat and throw in the tomatoes. Immediately place a lid on and leave for a few minutes till the crackling dies down.
- Remove the lid, stir in the butter and season with salt and pepper.
- Toss the spaghetti in the sauce and serve with grated Parmesan.

PREPARATION TIME: 5 MINUTES

COOKING TIME: 12 MINUTES

INGREDIENTS

500 g / 1 lb 2 oz / 4 ½ cups dried spaghetti
2 tbsp olive oil
2 cloves garlic, chopped
400 g / 14 oz / 2 cups chopped tomatoes
2 tbsp butter
2 tbsp Parmesan, grated to serve

Spaghetti in Mascarpone and Tomato Sauce

210

For a creamier sauce add 2 tbsp Mascarpone.

211

SERVES 4

Pasta with Mussels in Gorgonzola Sauce

Mussel Pasta with Lemon

212

Omit the Gorgonzola and use a little lemon juice and zest in the sauce.

Mussel Pasta with Red Pepper

213

Substitute a chopped leek for the red pepper.

Mussel Pasta with Feta

214

Substitute the Gorgonzola for the same amount of Feta cheese and cook the same.

PREPARATION TIME: 15 MINUTES

COOKING TIME: 12 MINUTES

INGREDIENTS

500 g / 1 lb 2 oz / 4 ½ cups farfalle pasta
1 tbsp butter
1 shallot, finely chopped
1 red pepper, deseeded and finely chopped
1 clove garlic, chopped
500 g / 1 lb 2 oz / 3 ⅓ cups mussels, cleaned
100 ml / 3 ½ fl. oz / ½ cup pastis
120 g / 4 ½ oz / ½ cup Gorgonzola
120 g / 4 ½ oz / ½ cup Mascarpone

- Cook the pasta in boiling salted water according to packet instructions. Once cooked, drain and toss with a little oil and keep warm.
- Meanwhile heat the butter in a large pan and add the shallot, pepper and garlic.
- Once softened add the mussels and pastis, allow to bubble up then cover with a lid and leave to simmer for about 5 minutes or until the mussels have opened.
- Carefully tip the mussels into a colander over a large bowl to collect the cooking liquor, leaving any sediment behind in the bottom and discarding any mussels that remain closed.
- Heat the Gorgonzola and Mascarpone in a pan then add a little of the reserved cooking liquor and season with black pepper.
- Remove the meat from most of the mussels and add to the pan with the pasta.
- Serve decorated with remaining mussel shells.

Spinach Cannelloni with Tomato Sauce

215

SERVES 4

- Preheat the oven to 180°C (160° fan) / 350F / gas 5.
- Heat the butter in a pan with oil and cook the garlic for 2 minutes. Add the spinach and nutmeg and stir and toss until the spinach is completely wilted.
- Spoon into a sieve and press down firmly with a wooden spoon to extract as much liquid as possible. Once done, finely chop the spinach and leave to cool in a bowl.
- Stir in the ricotta, Parmesan, seasoning and mix well.
- Spoon into the tubes or onto the lasagna sheets and roll up to make 12 cylinders. Layer on a greased dish.
- To make the tomato sauce, heat the oil in a pan and add the garlic and tomatoes. Leave to simmer, topped up with water, for 10 minutes, then add the basil and season with salt and pepper.
- Spoon over the cannelloni and bake for around 15 minutes until bubbling.

Mushroom Cannelloni

216

Use 250 g / 9oz / 2 ½ cups chopped mushrooms instead of the spinach.

PREPARATION TIME: 40 MINUTES

COOKING TIME: 15 MINUTES

INGREDIENTS

12 cannelloni tubes or 12 sheets lasagna

FOR THE FILLING
2 tbsp butter
Olive oil
2 cloves garlic, chopped
Nutmeg, grated to taste
1 kg / 2 lb 4 oz spinach leaves, wilted
400 g / 14 oz ricotta
2 tbsp Parmesan, grated

FOR THE TOMATO SAUCE:
2 tbsp olive oil
1 clove garlic, chopped
400 g / 14 oz / 2 cups chopped tomatoes
200 ml / 7 fl. oz / 1 cup water
1 tbsp basil, chopped

Tagliatelle with Salmon and Sun-dried Tomatoes

217

SERVES 4

- Cook the tagliatelle in boiling salted water according to packet instructions.
- Drain, reserving a small amount of the water, and toss with a half the olive oil.
- Cut the salmon into strips and tear the tomatoes into pieces. Place in a bowl with the chopped chervil and the remaining oil.
- Toss with the pasta, adding a little of the reserved water to lubricate the sauce.
- Season with salt and pepper and serve.

Tagliatelle with Salmon and Spinach

218

Add 400 g / 14 oz / 1 ½ cups spinach, wilted under a high heat with a 1 crushed clove of garlic.

PREPARATION TIME: 5 MINUTES

COOKING TIME: 4 MINUTES

INGREDIENTS

500 g / 1 lb 2 oz fresh tagliatelle pasta
4 tbsp olive oil
200 g / 7 oz / ¾ cup smoked salmon
100 g / 3 ½ oz / ½ cup sundried tomatoes
1 tbsp chervil, chopped

219

SERVES 4

Linguine with Salmon and Courgettes

PREPARATION TIME: 10 MINUTES

COOKING TIME: 15 MINUTES

INGREDIENTS

500 g / 1 lb 2 oz / 2 cups linguine
2 fillets smoked salmon, skin removed
2 courgettes (zucchini)
2 tbsp butter
200 ml / 7 fl. oz / ¾ cup double (heavy) cream
½ lemon, grated zest and juiced
1 tbsp basil, chopped

- Cook the pasta in boiling salted water according to packet instructions. Drain and toss with a little oil and keep warm.
- Meanwhile, gently flake the salmon into bite-size pieces.
- Slice the courgettes (zucchini) lengthways then cut into ribbons with a vegetable peeler.
- Heat the butter in a pan and cook the courgettes (zucchini) for 2-3 minutes until just tender.
- Stir in the cream, lemon zest and juice, basil, and then the salmon, stirring carefully. Season with salt and pepper
- Toss with the linguine and serve.

Linguine with Salmon and Asparagus

220

Add 2 handfuls cooked peas, 8 stalks cooked and chopped asparagus in the butter.

221

SERVES 4

Ravioli with Gorgonzola

PREPARATION TIME: 35 MINUTES

COOKING TIME: 5 MINUTES

INGREDIENTS

500 g / 1 lb 2 oz pasta dough (page 92) rolled into 2 sheets

FOR THE FILLING
10 walnuts
200 g / 7 oz / ¾ cup ricotta
3 tbsp olive oil
4 tbsp parsley, chopped
250 g / 9 oz Gorgonzola, piccante or dolce
2 ripe pears

- Lightly toast the walnuts in a pan until they start to darken. Place in a food processor and mix to a crumble.
- Stir into the ricotta with 1 tbsp oil, parsley and seasoning. Lay a sheet of pasta onto a floured work surface and place 1 tsp of the mixture at intervals along the sheet, leaving a 5cm / 2" gap between each mound. Brush around each mound with a little beaten egg.
- Top with the second sheet of pasta and press down lightly around each mound. Cut out or stamp out with a cutter and lay on a baking tray.
- Warm the serving plates on a low heat in the oven with chopped Gorgonzola so it starts to melt.
- Slice the pears into quarters and core. Squeeze over a few drops of lemon juice to prevent browning.
- Cook the ravioli in boiling salted water for 2 minutes, remove and drain on kitchen paper.
- Toss gently with the melted Gorgonzola and top with the pears.

Ravioli with Pine Nuts

222

Swap the walnuts for 10 pine nuts instead.

223

SERVES 4

Tagliatelle with Creamy Lemon Sauce

- Cook the pasta in boiling salted water according to packet instructions.
- Warm the crème fraiche in a pan with the lemon zest and juice, basil and season with salt and pepper.
- Toss the pasta in the sauce with a little of the pasta cooking water to lubricate.

PREPARATION TIME: 2 MINUTES

COOKING TIME: 5 MINUTES

INGREDIENTS

500 g / 1 lb 2 oz/ 2 cups fresh tagliatelle
250 ml / 9 fl. oz / 1 cup crème fraiche
1 lemon, grated zest and juiced
2 tbsp basil, chopped

Tagliatelle in Cream with Green Beans

 224

Add any spring green vegetable to the sauce or strips of smoked salmon

225

SERVES 4

Smoked Salmon and Pasta Salad

- Cook the pasta in boiling salted water according to packet instructions.
- Drain, toss with a little oil and leave to cool.
- Cut the salmon into fine strips and place in a bowl with onions and watercress. Add the pasta.
- Whisk together the oil, lemon zest and juice and season.
- Toss the salad with the dressing and serve immediately decorated with cornichons.

PREPARATION TIME: 10 MINUTES

COOKING TIME: 12 MINUTES

INGREDIENTS

300 g / 10 ½ oz / 1 ¼ cups penne pasta or similar
200 g / 7 oz / ¾ cup smoked salmon
4 spring onions (scallions), finely chopped
4 tbsp watercress, chopped
6 tbsp extra virgin olive oil
1 lemon, grated zest and juice
Cornichons, to decorate

Salmon and Pasta Salad with Asparagus

 226

Steam 8 stalks of asparagus and add to the salad.

Chicken Pasta Salad with Cheese Crouton

Turkey Pasta Salad

228

Use turkey breast, roasted for about 40 minutes, instead of the chicken.

Pasta Salad with Mozzarella

229

Substitute the goats' cheese for mozzarella instead.

Penne Pasta Salad

230

Replace the Fusilli pasta with the same amount of al-dente cooked Penne.

PREPARATION TIME: 15 MINUTES

COOKING TIME: 30 MINUTES

INGREDIENTS

2 chicken breasts, skin on
1 red pepper, deseeded and chopped
2 tbsp olive oil
300 g / 10 oz / 1 ½ cups fusilli pasta
½ lemon, juiced
Handful black olives
4 slices baguette, 1 cm / ½" thick
60 g / 2 oz / ½ cup goats' cheese log, sliced
Mixed salad, to serve

- Preheat the oven to 200°C / 400F / gas 6. Place the chicken and pepper in a roasting tin and drizzle with 1 tbsp oil and season. Roast for about 25 minutes or until the chicken is cooked through.
- Leave the chicken to cool slightly in the pan, then tear into shreds and place in a bowl with the pepper and olives. Squeeze over a little lemon juice.
- Meanwhile cook the pasta in boiling salted water according to packet instructions.
- Drain and toss with a little olive oil to prevent sticking then tip into the bowl with the chicken.
- Drizzle with the remaining extra virgin olive oil and season carefully. You may want more lemon juice.
- Toast the baguettes brushed with a little oil under a hot grill until lightly gold.
- Top with the goats' cheese and grill again until the cheese is bubbling.
- Serve with the chicken pasta salad and some mixed leaves on the side.

231

SERVES 4

Angel Hair Pasta with Parsley Sauce

- Cook the pasta in boiling salted water according to packet instructions.
- Drain, toss with a little oil and keep warm.
- Meanwhile, heat the butter in a pan and gently sweat the shallot and garlic without colouring.
- Stir in the parsley, season and then toss with the pasta.
- Serve with the Parmesan sprinkled over.

PREPARATION TIME: 5 MINUTES

COOKING TIME: 5 MINUTES

INGREDIENTS

500 g / 1 lb 2 oz / 2 cups angel hair pasta
4 tbsp butter
2 shallots, finely chopped
1 clove garlic, finely chopped
2 tbsp flat leaf parsley, finely chopped
4 tbsp Parmesan, grated

Pasta with Peas and Parsley Sauce   232

Add 250 g / 9 oz frozen peas to the pasta when cooking

233

SERVES 4-6

Tortellini with Spinach and Cream

- Mix the pasta ingredients then knead with your hands for 5 minutes until smooth and elastic. Cover with film and chill for 30 minutes.
- Heat the butter in a pan and sweat the onion and garlic .
- Add the spinach, wilt down then add the nutmeg. Stir in the ricotta, Parmesan and parsley and leave to cool.
- Using a pasta machine, roll out the dough into one even sheet. Cut into 10cm / 4" squares.
- Place 1 tsp of filling in the middle of each square, then fold one corner over to make a triangle.
- Press the edges lightly together, bringing the corners of the triangle in together to make a circular shape.
- To cook bring a large pan of salted water to the boil and cook for 3-4 minutes. Remove carefully with a slotted spoon and drain on kitchen paper.
- Gently warm the cream with a little seasoning and serve over the pasta with grated Parmesan.

PREPARATION TIME: 90 MINUTES

COOKING TIME: 10 MINUTES

INGREDIENTS

FOR THE PASTA
500 g / 1 lb 2 oz / 2 cups grade '00' flour
4 eggs
500 g / 1 lb 2 oz / 2 cups spinach leaves wilted, squeezed dry and cooled

FOR THE FILLING:
3 tbsp butter
½ onion, peeled and finely chopped
1 clove garlic, finely chopped
500 g / 1 lb 2 oz / 2 cups spinach leaves
nutmeg, grated
100 g / 3 ½ oz / ½ cup ricotta
2 tbsp Parmesan, grated
1 tbsp flat leaf parsley, chopped

FOR THE SAUCE
250 ml / 9 fl. oz / 1 cup double cream
Parmesan, grated

Tortellini with Spinach and Tomatoes   234

Add 12 halved cherry tomatoes to the sauce and cook the same.

SERVES 4

Vegetable and Chicken Fusilli

PREPARATION TIME 12 MINUTES

COOKING TIME 20 MINUTES

INGREDIENTS

500 g / 1 lb 2 oz / 2 cups fusilli pasta
½ head broccoli, separated into florets
100 g / 3 ½ oz / ½ cup peas
2 tbsp olive oil
2 chicken breasts, chopped
2 red peppers, deseeded and finely chopped
salt and pepper
300 ml / 10 ½ fl. oz / 1 ¼ cups double (heavy) cream
4 tbsp Parmesan, grated
basil, to garnish

- Preheat the oven to 200ºC (180º fan) / 400F / gas 6.
- Cook the pasta in boiling salted water according to packet instructions. Add the broccoli florets and peas about 4-5 minutes before the end of cooking time.
- Drain and toss with a little oil.
- Heat the oil in a pan and fry the chicken and peppers until soft and golden in patches. Season.
- Tip into a buttered baking dish with the pasta and vegetables and pour over the cream.
- Mix gently and season then scatter with the Parmesan.
- Bake in the oven for about 20 minutes until golden and bubbling.

Vegetable and Turkey Fusilli

236

Swap the chicken for the same amount of turkey for a lighter option.

237

SERVES 4

Spelt Pasta with Mediterranean Vegetables

- Cook the pasta in boiling salted water according to packet instructions. Drain and toss with a little oil then keep warm.
- Meanwhile heat the oil in a pan and fry the red onion very gently for about 15 minutes until very sweet and tender.
- Add the garlic and aubergine (eggplant) and cook for about 10 minutes, seasoning lightly, until the aubergine is cooked.
- Stir in the artichokes, thyme and cream and adjust the seasoning.
- Toss the pasta with the sauce and serve with grated Parmesan.

PREPARATION TIME: 10 MINUTES

COOKING TIME: 30 MINUTES

INGREDIENTS

500 g / 1 lb 2 oz / 2 cups spelt pasta shapes
2 tbsp olive oil
1 red onion, peeled and finely chopped
1 clove garlic, chopped
1 aubergine (eggplant), finely chopped
285 g / 10 oz / jar artichoke hearts, drained and halved
Handful thyme leaves
250 ml / 9 fl. oz / 1 cup double (heavy) cream
2 tbsp Parmesan, grated to serve

Spelt Pasta with Blushed Tomatoes

238

Add a handful of sun-blushed tomatoes with the artichokes

239

SERVES 4

Spirali Pasta with Parma Ham, Parmesan and Basil

- Cook the pasta in boiling salted water according to packet instructions. Drain, reserving a little of the cooking water and toss with a little oil.
- Heat the butter in a pan and add the Parma ham.
- Toss in the pasta and 2 tbsp water, then stir in the Parmesan and basil.
- Season with salt and pepper and serve.

PREPARATION TIME: 5 MINUTES

COOKING TIME: 15 MINUTES

INGREDIENTS

500 g / 1 lb 2 oz / 2 cups spirali pasta
3 tbsp butter
4 slices Parma ham, cut into fine strips
4 tbsp Parmesan
1 tbsp basil, chopped

Spirali Pasta with Bresaola

240

Substitute the Parma ham for 4 fine strips of bresaola ham.

241

SERVES 4

Fettuccine with Pesto

PREPARATION TIME: 5 MINUTES

COOKING TIME: 10 MINUTES

INGREDIENTS

500 g / 1 lb 2 oz / 2 cups fettuccine pasta

FOR THE PESTO SAUCE:
Small handful pine nuts
1 clove garlic, peeled and chopped
3 big handfuls basil leaves, chopped
2 tbsp Parmesan, grated
Olive oil
Parmesan, grated to serve

- Cook the pasta in boiling salted water according to packet instructions. Drain, reserving a little of the water.
- To make the pesto sauce, combine the first 4 pesto ingredients in a food processor until you have a rough paste or pound in a pestle and mortar. Drizzle in enough oil to make a loose sauce.
- Toss the pasta in the pesto, loosening with a little cooking water.
- Serve with extra Parmesan.

Fettuccine with Sun-dried Tomatoes

 242

Add a handful of finely chopped sun-dried tomatoes to the ingredients for the pesto.

243

SERVES 4

Tagliatelle with Chicken and Peas

PREPARATION TIME: 5 MINUTES

COOKING TIME: 10 MINUTES

INGREDIENTS

500 g / 1 lb 2 oz / 2 cups fresh tagliatelle
150 g / 5 oz / 2 / 3 cup frozen peas
2 tbsp butter
2 chicken breasts, skinned and sliced into strips
1 tbsp thyme or rosemary leaves, finely chopped
½ lemon, juiced
3 tbsp Parmesan, grated

- Heat the butter in a pan and fry the chicken until golden.
- Throw in the herbs, season with salt and pepper and set aside.
- Cook the pasta with the peas in boiling salted water according to packet instructions – they should take the same amount of time.
- Drain, reserving a little cooking water.
- Tip the pasta and peas into the chicken pan back on the heat, add a little water to lubricate.
- Stir well, squeeze over some lemon juice and stir in the Parmesan.

Tagliatelle with Mushrooms and Peas

244

Sauté 450 g / 1 lb sliced button mushrooms for 5 minutes and add to the pesto sauce.

245

SERVES 2

Tortellini in Tomato Sauce

Tortellini in Chilli Tomato Sauce

246

Add 1 chopped chilli to the sauce and cook the same.

Tortellini in Creamy Tomato Sauce

247

Add 2 tbsb of Mascarpone to the sauce.

Tortellini with Cherry Tomatoes

248

Instead of using tinned tomatoes, substitute with 12 halved cherry tomatoes.

PREPARATION TIME: 5 MINUTES

COOKING TIME: 15 MINUTES

INGREDIENTS

2 tbsp olive oil
1 onion, finely chopped
1 clove garlic, finely chopped
400 g / 14 oz / 2 cups chopped tomatoes
Handful thyme leaves
500 g / 1 lb 2 oz / 2 cups ready made fresh tortellini, such as ham and cheese or spinach and ricotta

Heat the oil in a pan and sweat the onion and garlic without colouring.

Add the tomatoes and a splash of water and simmer for 10 minutes, then stir in the thyme leaves and season.

Cook the pasta in boiling salted water according to packet instructions. Drain.

Toss the pasta with the sauce and serve.

249

SERVES 4

Maltagliata with Artichokes

Maltagliata with Lemon

250

Use fresh lemon zest and juice instead of preserved lemons.

Maltagliata with Wine

251

Add 75 ml / 3 fl. oz white wine to the frying pan and reduce until syrupy.

Maltagliata with Porcini Mushrooms

252

Add 450 g / 1 lb porcini mushrooms with the artichokes and cook the same.

PREPARATION TIME: 15 MINUTES

COOKING TIME: 35 MINUTES

INGREDIENTS

12 lasagna sheets
4 globe artichokes, prepared (see P) in acidulated water
2 confit lemons, quartered
2 tbsp olive oil

- Using a non-iron or aluminium pan, boil the artichokes in salted, acidulated water for about 30 minutes, or until one of the outer leaves pulls away easily.
- Drain and cut into quarters.
- Cut the lasagna sheets into irregular shapes (maltagliata means mal-formed in Italian).
- Cook in boiling salted water according to packet instructions. Drain.
- Heat the oil in a pan with the confit lemons and gently warm the artichokes through in the oil. Season with salt and pepper.
- Toss with the pasta shapes and serve.

253

SERVES 6

Conchiglie Stuffed with Crab

- Cook the pasta in boiling salted water according to packet instructions. Drain and toss with olive oil.
- Place the basil, garlic and pine nuts in a pestle and mortar and crush to make a paste then pour in enough oil to loosen.
- Add the crab and tomatoes to the pesto and mix gently. Season.
- Preheat the oven to 150ºC (130º fan) / 300F / gas 2.
- Stuff the pasta shells with the pesto mixture and place in a buttered baking dish.
- Pour the stock into the bottom of the dish and cover with foil.
- Bake for 10 minutes then serve.

PREPARATION TIME: 20 MINUTES

COOKING TIME : 20 MINUTES

INGREDIENTS

1 kg / 2 lb 4 oz / 4 cups giant conchiglie shells
300 g / 10 ½ oz crab meat
2 large bunches basil, chopped
75 g / 3 oz / 1/3 cup pine nuts
5 cloves of garlic, chopped
extra virgin olive oil
3 tomatoes, finely chopped
100 ml / 3 ½ fl oz / ½ cup vegetable stock
salt and pepper

254

SERVES 4

Tagliatelle with Tuna

- Preheat the oven to 200ºC (180º fan) / 400F / gas 6.
- Roast the peppers in oil and seasoning for about 20 minutes or until soft and sweet.
- Cook the pasta in boiling salted water according to packet instructions. Drain, reserving a little of the cooking water and tip into a bowl.
- Toss with the roasted peppers, a little of the roasting juices and a tbsp of cooking water.
- Flake in the tuna and basil and season then serve.

PREPARATION TIME : 5 MINUTES

COOKING TIME : 25 MINUTES

INGREDIENTS

500 g / 1 lb 2 oz / 2 cups tagliatelle
3 tbsp olive oil
3-4 red peppers, roughly chopped
salt and pepper
375 g / 13 oz cans tuna in olive oil, drained
½ bunch basil, chopped

255

SERVES 2

Ravioli with Mushrooms

PREPARATION TIME 5 MINUTES

COOKING TIME 20 MINUTES

....

INGREDIENTS

2 tbsp olive oil
200g / 6 ½ oz / ¾ cup mushrooms,
chopped
2 sprigs thyme
1 clove garlic, chopped
400g / 14 oz / 2 cups chopped
tomatoes
500g / 1lb / 2 cups ready made fresh
ravioli, such as wild mushroom
2 tbsp Parmesan, grated to serve

- Heat the oil in a pan and add the mushrooms with the thyme and garlic.
- Cook briskly until the liquid evaporates, season then add the tomatoes and a splash of water.
- Simmer for 10 minutes.
- Meanwhile cook the pasta in boiling salted water according to packet instructions.
- Drain then toss with the sauce and serve with Parmesan.

256

SERVES 4

Penne with Summer Vegetables

PREPARATION TIME: 10 MINUTES

COOKING TIME: 12 MINUTES

....

INGREDIENTS

500g / 1lb / 2 cups penne pasta
100g / 3 ½ oz / ½ cup peas
4 tomatoes, chopped
1 clove garlic, crushed
1 tbsp olive oil
100g / 3 ½ oz / ½ cup feta cheese

- Cook the pasta in boiling salted water according to packet instructions.
- Five minutes before the end of cooking, add the peas. When cooked, drain and toss with a little oil.
- Meanwhile drizzle the tomatoes with oil, toss with the garlic and seasoning and leave to macerate.
- Toss the hot pasta with the peas, macerated tomatoes and top with crumbled cold feta to serve.

Penne with Creamy Summer Vegetables

257

Add 2 tbsb mascarpone to the pasta for a creamier finish.

258

SERVES 4

Chicken and Spinach Pasta Salad

- Cook the pasta in boiling salted water according to packet instructions.
- Meanwhile whisk together the oil and vinegar and season with salt and pepper.
- Heat a frying pan until very hot, add a little oil and cook the chicken quickly until golden.
- Drain the pasta and toss in the dressing with the chicken and leave to cool.
- Once warm, stir in the spinach and serve with the cheese sprinkled over.

PREPARATION TIME: 10 MINUTES

COOKING TIME: 15 MINUTES

INGREDIENTS

300 g / 10 oz / 1 ¼ cups fusilli pasta
6 tbsp olive oil
1-2 tbsp red wine vinegar
2 chicken breasts, sliced
140 g / 5 oz / 4 ½ cups baby spinach leaves
100 g / 3 ½ oz / ½ cup Emmental cheese, grated

Chicken and Mushroom Pasta Salad

259

A handful button mushrooms sliced and fried make a good substitute for the chicken

260

SERVES 4

Macaroni with Blue Cheese Sauce

- Cook the pasta in boiling salted water according to packet instructions.
- Drain and toss with a little butter.
- Meanwhile heat the Mascarpone with the Gorgonzola, stirring until it melts.
- Season generous with black pepper.
- Toss the pasta with the sauce and serve.

PREPARATION TIME: 2 MINUTES

COOKING TIME: 12 MINUTES

INGREDIENTS

500 g / 1 lb / 2 cups macaroni pasta
1 tbsp butter
120 g / 4 ¼ oz / ½ cup Mascarpone
100 g / 3 ½ oz / ½ cup Gorgonzola, piccante or dolce

SERVES 4

Tagliatelle with Basil Cream Sauce

Tagliatelle with Basil and Tomatoes

262

Add 2 chopped tomatoes to the cream when warming through.

PREPARATION TIME: 5 MINUTES

COOKING TIME: 6 MINUTES

....

INGREDIENTS

500 g / 1lb / 2 cups tagliatelle
1 tbsp butter
200ml / 6 ½ fl. oz / ¾ cup crème fraiche
½ lemon, grated zest
2 tbsp basil leaves, chopped

- Cook the pasta in boiling salted water according to packet instructions.
- Drain and toss with butter.
- Meanwhile heat the cream with the lemon zest, basil and seasoning.
- Toss the pasta with the cream and serve.

263

SERVES 4

Linguine Bolognese

- Heat the oil in a pan and sweat the onion and garlic until soft.
- Add the pancetta and fry until the fat runs.
- Add the mince and break it up with a wooden spoon, stirring frequently until cooked.
- Season with salt and pepper, then add the tomatoes. Partially cover and simmer for 15 minutes.
- Meanwhile cook the pasta in boiling salted water according to packet instructions.
- Drain and toss with a little oil.
- Stir the parsley through the sauce, then toss the pasta in the sauce.
- Serve with grated Parmesan.

PREPARATION TIME: 15 MINUTES

COOKING TIME: 30 MINUTES

INGREDIENTS

500 g / 1 lb / 2 cups linguine
3 tbsp olive oil
2 onions, peeled and finely chopped
2 cloves garlic, peeled and finely chopped
1 pack pancetta or bacon lardons
500 g / 1 lb / 2 cups minced beef
800 g / 1 ¾ lbs / 4 cups chopped tomatoes
100 g / 3 ½ oz / ½ cup Parmesan, grated
2 tbsp parsley, chopped

Linguine Bolognese with Mushrooms

264

Add 450 g / 14 oz sliced button mushrooms to the sauce and cook the same.

265

SERVES 2

Pasta with Prawns and Coconut Milk

- Cook the pasta in boiling salted water according to packet instructions. Drain and toss with a little oil.
- Meanwhile heat the coconut milk in a pan and add the lemongrass and lime zest and leave to simmer for 5 minutes to infuse.
- Add the prawns and leave till they turn pink, then stir in the basil and season with salt and pepper.
- Fish out the lemongrass stalk.
- Toss through the pasta and serve.

PREPARATION TIME: 10 MINUTES

COOKING TIME: 15 MINUTES

INGREDIENTS

200 g / 6 ½ oz / ¾ cup spirali pasta
200 ml / 6 ¾ fl. oz / 1 cup coconut milk
1 stalk lemongrass, crushed
1 lime, grated zest
200 g / 7 oz / 2 / 3 cup raw prawns (shrimps), shelled
1 tbsp basil, chopped

Pasta with Mussels and Coconut

266

Add 250 g cooked mussels to the coconut milk along with a little of the mussel cooking juice.

267

SERVES 4

Spinach Tagliatelle with Smoked Trout

PREPARATION TIME: 5 MINUTES

COOKING TIME: 12 MINUTES

INGREDIENTS

500 g / 1 lb / 2 cups spinach
tagliatelle
300 g / 10 oz / 1 ¼ cups smoked trout
1 pack rocket (arugula)
1 tbsp olive oil
Parmesan shavings

- Cook the pasta in boiling salted water according to packet instructions.
- Flake the trout and chop the rocket (arugula).
- When cooked, drain the pasta, not too thoroughly, and toss with oil.
- Stir through the trout and rocket, season and serve with Parmesan shavings.

Spinach Tagliatelle with Cod

268

Use a cod fillet, cooked in the oven for 8 minutes, then flake into the pasta.

269

SERVES 4

Three Cheese Orecchiette

PREPARATION TIME: 10 MINUTES

COOKING TIME: 15 MINUTES

INGREDIENTS

500 g / 1 lb / 2 cups orecchiette
200 ml / 6 ½ fl. oz / ¾ cup double
(heavy) cream
50 g / 2 oz / ⅓ cup Mimolette cheese,
grated
50 g / 2 oz / ⅓ cup Parmesan, grated
50 g / 2 oz / ⅓ cup Gruyere or
fontina, grated

- Cook the orecchiette in boiling salted water according to packet instructions.
- Warm the cream and stir in the cheeses until they melt.
- Season generously with black pepper and a little salt.
- Drain the pasta and toss through the sauce. Serve.

Three Cheese Orecciette with Tomatoes

270

Add 2 chopped tomatoes just at the end of the sauce.

271

SERVES 4

Penne with Green and Black Olives

- Cook the pasta in boiling salted water according to packet instructions.
- Meanwhile heat the olive oil in a pan until quite hot, throw in the garlic and the tomatoes tomatoes. Cover with a lid as it will spit.
- When the spitting dies down, remove the lid and stir in the basil and olives, season and remove from the heat.
- Drain the pasta and toss with the sauce.
- Serve with grated Parmesan

PREPARATION TIME: 5 MINUTES

COOKING TIME: 12 MINUTES

INGREDIENTS

500 g / 1 lb / 2 cups penne pasta
2 tbsp olive oil
1 clove garlic, finely sliced
800 g / 1 ¾ lbs / 4 cups chopped tomatoes
2 tbsp basil, whole leaves
1 handful mixed green and black olives
4 tbsp Parmesan, to serve

Penne with Sun-dried Tomatoes   272

Replace the olives for 100 g / 3 ½ oz / ½ cup of sun-dried tomatoes.

273

SERVES 4

Orecchiette with Apples, Spinach and Parma Ham

- Cook the pasta in boiling salted water according to packet instructions.
- Meanwhile heat the butter and cook the apple until just tender but holding its shape.
- Add the Parma ham and remove from the heat.
- Drain the pasta, reserving some of the cooking water.
- Toss the pasta with the apples and ham, adding a tbsp of cooking water to lubricate. Season with salt and pepper.
- Toss through the spinach leaves, add the Pecorino and serve.

PREPARATION TIME: 10 MINUTES

COOKING TIME: 14 MINUTES

INGREDIENTS

500 g / 1 lb / 2 cups orecchiette pasta
2 tbsp butter
1 eating apple, peeled, quartered, cored and sliced
8 slices Parma ham, chopped
2 handfuls baby spinach leaves
2 tbsp Pecorino, grated

Orrecchiette with Spinach and Bresaola   274

Substitute the same amount of Parma ham with bresaola.

275

SERVES 4

Farfalle with Spicy Cherry Tomatoes

- Cook the pasta in boiling salted water according to packet instructions.
- Heat the olive oil in a pan and add the garlic and sage leaves. Fry the sage leaves till crisp, then remove from the pan and drain on kitchen paper.
- Add the tomatoes and toss in the flavoured oil until just tender, then sprinkle with Tabasco to taste. Season with salt and pepper and remove from the heat.
- Drain the pasta – not too thoroughly – then toss with the tomatoes and sage leaves.
- Serve with more Tabasco if desired.

PREPARATION TIME: 5 MINUTES

COOKING TIME: 12 MINUTES

INGREDIENTS

500 g / 1 lb / 2 cups farfalle pasta
2 tbsp olive oil
2 cloves garlic, finely chopped
1 tbsp sage leaves, chopped
300 g / 10 oz / 1 ¼ cups cherry tomatoes, halved
Tabasco, to taste

Tagliatelle with Leeks

276

SERVES 4

PREPARATION TIME 10 MINUTES

COOKING TIME 20 MINUTES

INGREDIENTS

500g / 1 lb / 2 cups tagliatelle
3 tbsp butter
2 leeks, trimmed and finely sliced

2 sprigs thyme
300ml / 10 fl oz / 1 ¼ cups passata

- Cook the pasta in boiling salted water according to packet instructions.
- Drain and toss with a little oil.
- Meanwhile heat the butter in a pan and add the leeks and thyme with a little salt. Cook very gently until soft and sweet.
- Add the passata and leave to simmer for 10 minutes.
- Adjust the seasoning in the sauce.
- Drain the pasta and toss with the sauce before serving.

Faggottini Pasta with Basil Cream

277

SERVES 4

PREPARATION TIME: 5 MINUTES

COOKING TIME: 6 MINUTES

INGREDIENTS

500 g / 1lb / 2 cups faggottini pasta
1 tbsp butter
200 ml / 6 ½ fl. oz / ¾ cup crème fraiche

½ lemon, grated zest
2 tbsp basil leaves, chopped

- Cook the pasta in boiling salted water according to packet instructions.
- Drain and toss with butter.
- Meanwhile heat the cream with the lemon zest, basil and seasoning.
- Toss the pasta with the cream and serve.

278
SERVES 4
Spaghetti with Mussels and Tomato

- Cook the pasta in boiling salted water according to packet instructions. When cooked, drain and toss with a little oil.
- Meanwhile place the mussels in a large pan with a splash of water and cook over a medium heat for 5 minutes or until the mussels have opened.
- Drain in a colander over a bowl, then leave to cool.
- Once cool, remove the mussel meat from the shells, reserving a few for decoration.
- Heat the olive oil in a pan and cook the shallot and garlic gently. Add the chilli flakes if using.
- Add the tomatoes and a splash of the mussel cooking liquor and leave to simmer for 10 minutes.
- Add the mussels to the sauce then toss with the spaghetti. Stir in the basil, season and serve decorated with the reserved shells.

Spaghetti with Prawns and Tomato
279

Add 300 g / 10 oz / 1 cup raw prawns to the sauce just before the end of cooking.

PREPARATION TIME: 15 MINUTES

COOKING TIME: 30 MINUTES

INGREDIENTS

500 g / 1 lb / 2 cups spaghetti
500 g / 1 lb / 2 cups mussels, cleaned
2 tbsp olive oil
1 shallot, finely chopped
2 cloves garlic, sliced
Pinch dried chilli flakes (optional)
400 g / 14 oz / 2 cups chopped tomatoes
1 tbsp basil, chopped

280
SERVES 4
Bollito Misto

- Place the chicken in a large stock pot with the celery, carrots and parsley stalks. Cover with water and bring to a gentle simmer,.
- Reduce the heat and poach for 45 minutes. Remove from the liquid and keep warm.
- Add the tongue and salt beef and poach for 3 hours.
- After 2 hours 30 minutes, wrap the cotechino sausage in foil and add to the pot for the last 30 minutes.
- Chop all the ingredients together, adding the oil to make a loose sauce.
- Remove the meats and vegetables from the stock pot and discard the vegetables.
- Add the carrots and celery back to the pot and boil until tender. Remove when cooked through.
- Slice the meats onto a large platter and moisten with the hot stock. Arrange the carrots and celery around. Serve the sauces and lentils alongside.

Meaty Bollito Misto
281

This stew is all about big flavours. Try poaching pig's trotter, marrowbone or silverside of veal.

PREPARATION TIME: 30 MINUTES

**COOKING TIME:
3 HOURS 45 MINUTES**

INGREDIENTS

1 chicken
1 head of celery, roughly chopped
4 carrots, roughly chopped
handful parsley stalks
1 calf's tongue, prepped for cooking
500 g / 1 lb salt beef brisket
1 cotechino sausage (spicy Italian)

FOR THE SALSA VERDE
2 tbsp parsley, chopped
2 tbsp basil, chopped
2 tbsp mint, chopped
1 tbsp Dijon mustard
2 tsp capers, drained
6 anchovies, drained and chopped
1 tbsp red wine vinegar
250 ml / 9 fl. oz / 1 cup olive oil
4 carrots, peeled and sliced
1 head of celery, sliced
100 g / 3 ½ oz / ½ cup Puy lentils
200 ml / 6 ½ fl. oz / ¾ cup stock

282

SERVES 4-6

Lasagna

PREPARATION TIME: 2 HOURS

COOKING TIME: 50 MINUTES

....

INGREDIENTS

150 ml / 5 fl. oz / 2 / 3 cup beef stock
12 lasagna sheets
2 tbsp Parmesan, grated

FOR THE TOMATO SAUCE

1 tbsp olive oil
1 onion, peeled and finely chopped
2 celery stalks, finely chopped
2 cloves garlic, finely chopped
2 carrots, peeled and thickly sliced
2 courgettes (zucchini), thickly sliced
120 g / 4 oz / ½ cup pancetta, cubed
500 g / 1 lb / 2 ¼ cups minced beef
120 ml / 4 fl. oz / ½ cup white wine
800 g / 1 ¾ lbs oz / 4 cups tomatoes
550 ml / 1 pint / 2 cups beef stock

FOR THE BÉCHAMEL SAUCE

2 tbsp butter
2 tbsp plain (all-purpose) flour
700 ml / 1 ¼ pints / 2 ¾ cups milk
1 bay leaf
nutmeg, grated

- To make the tomato sauce, fry the chopped vegetables, carrots, courgettes and pancetta in oil for 10 minutes.
- Add the beef, breaking it up with a wooden spoon until cooked through. Season with salt and pepper.
- Add the wine and tomatoes and leave to simmer for 2 hours, adding more stock as it absorbs.
- Heat the butter in a pan, then stir in the flour to make a roux. Whisk in the milk a little at a time.
- Add the bay leaf and simmer for 10 minutes, whisking frequently until thick. Season and add grated nutmeg.
- Preheat the oven to 190°C (170° fan) / 375F / gas 5. Add 4 sheets of lasagna to a baking dish and add a third of the Bolognese sauce in the bottom of a baking dish, then a quarter of the béchamel.
- Repeat twice more, then cover the top layer of lasagna with béchamel and sprinkle over the parmesan.
- Bake in the oven for 40 minutes until the pasta is tender. Leave to rest for 10 minutes before serving.

Spinach Lasagna

 283

Use green spinach lasagna sheets instead of plain and cook in the same way.

284

MAKES 4

Spaghetti and Bacon Fritters

PREPARATION TIME: 15 MINUTES

COOKING TIME: 10 MINUTES

....

INGREDIENTS

200 g / 6 ½ oz / ¾ cup spaghetti
4 rashers bacon or pancetta, finely chopped
2 cloves garlic, finely chopped
1 tbsp parsley, finely chopped
2 eggs + 1 egg yolk
3 tbsp Parmesan, grated
3 tbsp olive oil

- Cook the pasta in boiling salted water according to packet instructions.
- Cook the bacon in 1 tbsp of oil until golden.
- Mix together the garlic, parsley, eggs and Parmesan, then stir in the bacon.
- Drain the pasta and leave to cool, then roughly chop into shorter lengths.
- Heat 2 tbsp oil in a pan (the bacon one for preference) and then spoon dollops of the spaghetti mixture into the pan.
- Fry until golden and crisp on both sides. Serve hot.

Spaghetti and Chilli Fritters

 285

Add 1 tsp of dried chilli flakes.

Spaghetti and Anchovy Fritters

 286

Omit the bacon and use 3 anchovies, finely chopped

287

SERVES 4

Conchiglie with Asparagus and Beef

Conchiglie with Ham 288

Use any kind of cured ham instead of the beef

Conchiglie with Rocket 289

Use rocket (arugala) or watercress instead of asparagus, wilted in the butter

Conchiglie with Green Beans 290

Substitute the Asparagus with the same amount of green beans.

PREPARATION TIME: 10 MINUTES

COOKING TIME: 12 MINUTES

INGREDIENTS

500 g / 1 lb / 2 cups conchiglie pasta
8 stalks asparagus, woody ends snapped off and cut into short lengths
60 g / 2 oz / ¼ cup butter
1 clove garlic, sliced
¼ lemon, grated zest
8 slices air-dried beef, sliced into strips

- Cook the pasta in boiling salted water according to packet instructions.
- Add the asparagus 3 minutes before the end of the cooking time.
- Meanwhile heat the butter and garlic in a pan, then add the beef and zest and toss together.
- Drain the pasta, reserving a little of the water and toss with the butter sauce, adding 1-2 tbsp of reserved cooking water to amalgamate the sauce.
- Season and serve.

291

SERVES 4

Beef Cannelloni

PREPARATION TIME: 20 MINUTES

COOKING TIME: 30 MINUTES

INGREDIENTS

12 cannelloni tubes
550 ml / 1 pint / 2 cups passata
2 balls mozzarella, sliced

FOR THE FILLING
1 tbsp butter
1 tbsp olive oil
1 onion, peeled and finely chopped
2 celery stalks, finely chopped
2 cloves garlic, finely chopped
2 carrots, finely chopped
500 g / 1 lb / 2 cups minced beef
120 ml / 4 fl. oz / ½ cup dry white wine

- Preheat the oven to 190°C / 375F / gas 5.
- To make the filling, heat the butter with the oil and cook the vegetables until soft.
- Add the beef and break it down with a wooden spoon, stirring until it is cooked through.
- Add the white wine and season with salt and pepper, allowing the alcohol from the wine to evaporate.
- Use a teaspoon to fill the cannelloni tubes with the beef mixture then lay in a greased baking dish.
- Pour over the passata and lay the mozzarella slices over the pasta.
- Bake in the oven for 25-30 minutes until bubbling and golden.

Pork Cannelloni

292

Use the same amount of minced pork instead of beef.

293

SERVES 4

Faggottini with Basil

PREPARATION TIME: 25 MINUTES

COOKING TIME: 2 MINUTES

INGREDIENTS

500 g / 1 lb recipe pasta (see p.) rolled into 2 sheets

FOR THE FILLING
1 large bunch basil, chopped
200 g / 6 ½ oz / ¾ cup ricotta
1 tbsp olive oil
60 g / 2 oz / ⅓ cup butter
Basil sprigs
½ lemon, grated zest

- Stir the basil into the ricotta with a little oil and seasoning.
- Lay a sheet of pasta onto a floured work surface and place teaspoonfuls of the mixture at intervals along the sheet, leaving a 5cm / 2" gap between each mound. Brush around each mound with a little beaten egg.
- Top with the second sheet of pasta and press down lightly around each mound, pressing out all the air. Cut out or stamp out with a crinkled cutter and lay on a baking tray.
- Repeat and then cover the ravioli with a damp tea towel until ready to cook.
- Cook the ravioli in boiling salted water for 2 minutes, removing with a slotted spoon and drain on kitchen paper.
- Toss gently with the melted butter and top with basil leaves and lemon zest.

Faggottini with Sun-dried Tomatoes

294

Add 100 g / 3 ½ oz / ½ cup sun-dried tomatoes at the end.

295

SERVES 4

Lasagna with Ceps

- Heat the butter with a little oil in a pan and add the finely chopped vegetables, the mushrooms and pancetta and cook for about 10 minutes.
- Add the beef, wine and the tomatoes and half the stock and then lower the heat. Partially cover and leave to simmer for 2 hours, adding more stock as it absorbs.
- To make the béchamel, heat the butter in a pan then stir in the flour to make a paste. Whisk in the milk a little at a time. Add the bay leaf and simmer for 10 minutes, whisking frequently until thick. Season and add a little freshly grated nutmeg.
- Preheat the oven to 190°C (170° fan) / 375F / gas 5. Add 4 lasagna sheets then a third of the filling in the bottom of a baking dish, then a quarter of the béchamel.
- Repeat twice more, then cover the top with béchamel and sprinkle over the Parmesan. Bake in the oven for 40 minutes. Leave to rest for 10 minutes before serving.

Lasagna with Courgette

296

Substitute the ceps for 2 courgettes, finely chopped, and cook in the same way.

PREPARATION TIME: 2 HOURS

COOKING TIME: 2 HOURS 40 MINUTES

INGREDIENTS

150 ml / 5 fl. oz / 2 / 3 cup beef stock
12 lasagna sheets
2 tbsp Parmesan, grated

FOR THE FILLING

1 tbsp butter
2 tbsp olive oil
1 onion, peeled and finely chopped
2 celery stalks, finely chopped
2 cloves garlic, finely chopped
2 carrots, finely chopped
200 g / 6 ½ oz / ¾ cup mushrooms
120 g / 4 oz / ½ cup pancetta, cubed
500 g / 1 lb / 2 cups minced beef
120 ml / 4 fl. oz / ½ cup white wine
800 g / 1 ¾ lbs / 4 cups tomatoes
450 ml / 1 pint / 2 cups beef stock

FOR THE BÉCHAMEL SAUCE

2 tbsp butter
2 tbsp plain (all-purpose) flour
700 ml / 1 ¼ pints / 2 ¾ cups milk
1 bay leaf, nutmeg, grated to taste

297

SERVES 4-6

Green Pesto Pasta Salad

- Cook the pasta in boiling, salted water according to packet instructions.
- Drain, then toss with oil and leave to cool.
- Meanwhile heat the oil in a pan and fry the ham until crisp – 2-3 minutes. Remove and drain on kitchen paper.
- Toss the just warm pasta with the pesto and a little of the oil from the ham and season.
- Serve sprinkled with Parmesan and decorated with prosciutto.

PREPARATION TIME: 5 MINUTES

COOKING TIME: 12 MINUTES

INGREDIENTS

500 g / 1 lb / 2 cups penne pasta
2 tbsp olive oil
6 slices prosciutto ham
6 tbsp pesto
2 tbsp Parmesan, grated

Red Pesto Pasta Salad

298

Use red pesto instead of green.

299

SERVES 4

Pasta with Pesto and Salmon

PREPARATION TIME: 10 MINUTES

COOKING TIME: 15 MINUTES

INGREDIENTS

500 g / 1 lb / 2 cups penne pasta
2 tbsp olive oil
1 courgette (zucchini), thinly sliced
2 salmon steaks, cooked
Handful black olives, pitted and chopped
2 tomatoes, finely chopped
4 tbsp pesto

- Cook the pasta in boiling salted water according to packet instructions. Drain, reserving a little of the cooking water.
- Meanwhile heat the oil in a pan and cook the courgette (zucchini) until tender.
- Flake the salmon into large chunks and mix with the chopped olives and tomatoes. Stir in the courgettes.
- Add to the pan with the drained pasta, the pesto and a little cooking water to loosen the sauce.
- Season with salt and pepper and serve.

Pasta with Pesto and Cod

300

Use 1 cod fillet, cooked in the oven for 8 minutes on 180°C (160° fan) 350F / gas 4 for 8 minutes, then sprinkle into the pasta.

301

SERVES 4

Chicken Lasagna

PREPARATION TIME:
1 HOUR 15 MINUTES

COOKING TIME: 1 HOUR 40 MINUTES

INGREDIENTS

150 ml / 5 fl. oz / 2 / 3 cup beef stock
12 lasagna sheets, pre-cooked
2 tbsp Parmesan, grated

FOR THE SAUCE
1 tbsp butter
1 tbsp olive oil
1 onion, peeled and finely chopped
2 celery stalks, finely chopped
2 cloves garlic, finely chopped
2 carrots, finely chopped
120 g / 4 oz / ½ cup pancetta, cubed
500 g / 1 lb chicken breast, chopped
120 ml / 4 fl. oz / ½ cup white wine
800 g / 1 ¾ lbs / 4 cups tomatoes

FOR THE BÉCHAMEL SAUCE
2 tbsp butter
2 tbsp plain (all purpose) flour
700 ml / 1 ¼ pints / 2 ¾ cups milk
1 bay leaf
nutmeg, grated

- To make the tomato sauce, heat the butter with a little oil in a pan and add the finely chopped vegetables and pancetta and cook for about 10 minutes.
- Add the chicken and cook until golden. Season with salt and pepper. Add the wine and tomatoes and simmer for about 45 minutes.
- Make the béchamel by heating the butter in a pan until foaming, then stirring in the flour to make a paste.
- Whisk in the milk a little at a time. Add the bay leaf and simmer for 10 minutes, whisking frequently until thick. Season and add a little freshly grated nutmeg.
- Preheat the oven to 190°C (170° fan) / 375F / gas 5. Lay 4 lasagna sheets followed by a third of the Bolognese sauce in the bottom of a baking dish, then a quarter of the béchamel. Repeat twice more, then cover the top layer with béchamel and sprinkle over the Parmesan.
- Bake in the oven for 40 minutes. Leave to rest for 10 minutes before serving.

Turkey Lasagna

302

Use the same amount of turkey breast instead of chicken

SERVES 4

Farfalle with Chicken and Vegetables

Farfalle with Aubergine

304

Use ½ aubergine (eggplant), diced in addition to the vegetables

Farfalle with Prawns

305

Change the chicken for prawns.

Farfalle with Green Pepper

306

Substitute the red peppers for 2 green peppers.

PREPARATION TIME: 10 MINUTES

COOKING TIME: 25 MINUTES

INGREDIENTS

500 g / 1 lb / 2 cups farfalle
2 tbsp olive oil
1 onion, peeled and sliced
2 chicken breasts, chopped
140 g / 5 oz / ½ jar artichoke hearts
2 red peppers, 'cheeks' cut off
1 sprig oregano

- Cook the pasta in boiling salted water according to packet instructions. Drain, reserving a little of the water.
- Heat the oil in a pan and cook the onion for about 15 minutes until soft and sweet.
- Add the chicken and peppers and cook briskly until golden.
- Add the artichokes and oregano and season with salt and pepper.
- Toss the pasta with the chicken, adding a little cooking water to lubricate.
- Serve hot.

307

SERVES 4

Fusilli with Bacon

- Cook the pasta in boiling salted water according to packet instructions.
- Drain, reserving a little of the cooking water.
- Meanwhile cook the pancetta in the butter until golden.
- Throw in the tarragon leaves and 2 tbsp cooking water, then toss with the pasta.
- Season carefully and serve.

PREPARATION TIME 2 HOURS

COOKING TIME 10 MINUTES

INGREDIENTS

500g / 1 lb / 2 cups fusilli pasta
60g / 2 oz / ¼ cup butter
80g / 3 oz / 1/3 cup diced pancetta or smoked bacon
½ bunch tarragon leaves, chopped
Salt and pepper

Salmon and Spinach Gratin

308

SERVES 4

PREPARATION TIME 12 MINUTES

COOKING TIME 25 MINUTES

INGREDIENTS

500g / 1 lb / 2 cups penne
150g / 5 oz / 2/3 cup smoked salmon, chopped

250g / 9 oz / 1 cup spinach leaves, chopped
400ml / 13 ½ fl oz / 1 ½ cups double (heavy) cream
Zest of 1 lemon
Salt and pepper
2 tbsp Parmesan, grated

- Preheat the oven to 200C / 400F / gas 7.
- Cook the pasta in boiling salted water according to packet instructions.
- Drain and place in a gratin or baking dish.
- Toss the salmon, spinach and lemon zest with the pasta, then pour over the cream. Season well.
- Sprinkle over the Parmesan and bake in the oven for about 25 minutes until golden and bubbling..

Ricotta Spinach Cannelloni

309

SERVES 4

PREPARATION TIME: 40 MINUTES

COOKING TIME: 15 MINUTES

INGREDIENTS

2 tbsp butter
1 tbsp olive oil
2 cloves garlic, chopped
Nutmeg, grated to taste

1 kg / 2 lbs / 4 ½ cups spinach leaves
400g / 13 ½ oz / 1 ½ cups ricotta
2 tbsp Parmesan, grated
12 cannelloni tubes
For the tomato sauce
2 tbsp olive oil
1 clove of garlic, chopped
2 x 400g can chopped tomatoes
½ bunch basil, chopped

- Preheat the oven to 180C / 350F / gas 5. To make the filling, heat the butter in a large pan with the oil and cook the garlic for 2 minutes.
- Add the spinach and nutmeg and stir and toss until the spinach is completely wilted.
- Spoon into a sieve and press down firmly with a wooden spoon to extract as much liquid as possible. Once done, finely chop the spinach and leave to cool in a bowl.
- Stir in the ricotta, Parmesan and seasoning and mix well.
- Spoon into the tubes or onto the lasagna sheets and roll up to make 12 cylinders, then lay in a greased baking dish.
- To make the tomato sauce, heat the oil in a pan and add the garlic and tomatoes. Leave to simmer, topped up with ½ a can of water, for 10 minutes, then add the basil and season.
- Spoon over the cannelloni and bake for around 15 minutes until bubbling.

310

SERVES 4

Tagliatelle with Vegetables and Cream

- Heat the butter in a pan and sweat the shallot and garlic without colouring.
- Once softened, add the diced courgette and pepper and cook until tender.
- Cook the pasta in boiling salted water according to packet instructions. Drain and toss with a little oil.
- Add the cream to the vegetables and season well.
- Toss the pasta with the cream sauce and serve with Parmesan.

PREPARATION TIME: 10 MINUTES

COOKING TIME: 10 MINUTES

....

INGREDIENTS

500g / 1 lb / 2 cups tagliatelle
1 tbsp butter
1 shallot, finely chopped
1 clove of garlic, finely chopped
1 courgette, diced
1 red pepper, deseeded and diced
400ml / 13 ½ fl oz / 1 ½ cups double (heavy) cream or creme fraiche
Salt and pepper
3 tbsp Parmesan, grated

311

SERVES 4

Cannelloni wrapped in Coppa

- Plunge the tomatoes into boiling water and leave for 30 seconds. Remove and peel away the skin. Deseed and dice the flesh.
- Mix the tomato concasse in a bowl with 1 tbsp olive oil, salt and pepper. Stir in the basil and chives and ricotta. Taste and adjust the seasoning if necessary.
- Cook the cannelloni tubes in boiling salted water for 10 minutes. Drain and pat dry.
- Working quickly, use a teaspoon or piping bag to stuff the tubes with equal amounts of filling.
- Wrap the tubes in a slice of coppa and serve.

PREPARATION TIME 20 MINUTES

COOKING TIME 10 MINUTES

....

INGREDIENTS

3 tomatoes
500g / 1 lb / 2 cups ricotta
½ bunch basil, chopped
1 bunch chives, finely chopped
Salt and pepper
12 cannelloni tubes
12 slices Coppa ham
Olive oil

312

SERVES 4

Leek, Trout and Cheese Bake

PREPARATION TIME 10 MINUTES

COOKING TIME 20 MINUTES

INGREDIENTS

12 lasagna sheets
200g / 6 ½ oz / ¾ cup smoked trout fillets
300ml / 10 fl oz / 1 ¼ cups creme fraiche
½ bunch dill, finely chopped
Zest and juice of ½ lemon
Salt and pepper
40g / 1 oz butter
4 leeks, trimmed and finely sliced

- Cook the pasta in boiling salted water according to packet instructions.
- Drain, brush over a little oil and keep warm.
- Cook the leeks very gently in the butter with a sprinkling of salt until very soft and sweet.
- Meanwhile flake the trout fillets, removing any bones, into a bowl.
- Gently mix with the creme fraiche, dill, lemon zest and a little juice. Season well.
- Layer the lasagna sheets onto plates, 3 per serving. Spoon over the trout and creme fraiche filling, then top with leeks, then another layer of pasta and repeat.
- Serve drizzled with extra virgin olive oil.

313

SERVES 2

Ravioli with Roquefort

PREPARATION TIME 5 MINUTES

COOKING TIME 8 MINUTES

INGREDIENTS

250 g fresh ready-made ravioli, wild mushroom flavour
100g / 3 ½ oz / ½ cup Roquefort
250ml / 9 fl oz / 1 cup double cream
pinch curry powder
salt and pepper
2 tbsp walnuts, chopped

- Cook the pasta in boiling salted water according to packet instructions.
- Meanwhile heat the cream in a pan with the Roquefort and a small pinch curry powder. Season carefully.
- When the pasta is cooked, drain and toss with sauce.
- Scatter the walnuts over to serve.

314

SERVES 4

Penne with Spring Vegetables

Penne with Flageolet Beans

315

Use a can of flageolet beans, drained instead of the broad beans.

Penne with Green Beans

316

Use ½ a pack of green beans, chopped, instead of the broad beans.

Penne with Parma Ham

317

Omit the Pancetta for 4 slices of Parma ham.

PREPARATION TIME: 10 MINUTES

COOKING TIME: 15 MINUTES

INGREDIENTS

500 g / 1lb / 2 cups penne pasta
2 tbsp butter, or olive oil
100 g / 3 ½ oz / ½ cup broad beans, double podded
185 g / 6 ½ oz / 1 jar preserved artichokes, drained and halved
8 asparagus stalks, woody ends snapped off and cut into short lengths
4 slices pancetta

- Cook the pasta in boiling salted water according to packet instructions.
- Meanwhile heat the butter or oil in a pan and add the vegetables with a splash of pasta cooking water.
- Cook gently until the asparagus is just tender.
- Drain the pasta and toss with the vegetables and keep warm.
- Fry the pancetta slices in the pan until crisp and golden.
- Serve on top of the pasta.

318
SERVES 4

Spaghetti with Bass and Leek

Bass with Spinach Spaghetti   319

Replace the leeks with spinach or sorrel leaves

White Fish Spaghetti   320

Any firm white fish fillets would work with this dish.

PREPARATION TIME 10 MINUTES

COOKING TIME 15 MINUTES

INGREDIENTS

4 fillets of seabass, boned, skin on
500 g / 1 lb / 2 cups spaghetti
4 tbsp butter
2 leeks, trimmed and finely sliced
salt and pepper
juice of ½ lemon

- Cook the pasta in boiling salted water according to packet instructions.
- Drain and toss with a little butter.
- Meanwhile heat the butter in a pan and cook the leeks very slowly until sweet and soft. Season.
- Drizzle the bass with a little oil and fry skin side down for 3 minutes or until the skin is crisp.
- Turn the bass over and cook for a further 2-3 minutes or until just cooked through.
- Toss the spaghetti with the leeks and a little lemon juice, then serve topped with the bass fillets.

321

SERVES 4

Quadrucci with Double Tomato Sauce

- Preheat the oven to 200°C / 400F / gas 6.
- Drizzle the cherry tomatoes with oil, season and roast in the oven for 15 minutes or until softened and starting to blacken.
- Meanwhile heat 2 tbsp oil in a pan and cook the garlic and rosemary for 1 minute.
- Add the tomatoes and season and leave to simmer for 10 minutes.
- Cook the pasta in boiling salted water according to packet instructions. Drain, adding 2 tbsp water to the tomato sauce.
- Toss the pasta with the tomato sauce and serve the roasted tomatoes along side.

If you can't find quadrucci pasta, simply cut spinach lasagna sheets into squares and proceed as above.

PREPARATION TIME: 10 MINUTES

COOKING TIME: 20 MINUTES

INGREDIENTS

500 g / 1 lb / 2 cups spinach quadrucci pasta*
1 tbsp olive oil
300 g / 10 oz / 1 ¼ cups cherry tomatoes
2 cloves garlic, finely chopped
1 tbsp rosemary leaves, finely chopped
400 g / 14oz / 2 cups chopped tomatoes

Quadrucci with Spicy Sauce

322

Add 1 red chilli, finely chopped with the garlic.

323

SERVES 4

Tuna linguine

- Preheat the oven to 200°C / 400F / gas 6.
- Drizzle the tomatoes with oil, season and roast in the oven for 20 minutes until blackened and soft.
- Meanwhile cook the pasta in boiling salted water according to packet instructions.
- Drain and toss with a little oil.
- Flake the tuna into the tomatoes with the capers and parsley and pour everything over the pasta.
- Serve hot.

PREPARATION TIME: 10 MINUTES

COOKING TIME: 20 MINUTES

INGREDIENTS

500 g / 1 lb / 2 cups linguine
300 g / 10 z / 1 ¼ cups cherry tomatoes
1 tbsp olive oil
185 g / 6 ½ oz / ¾ cup canned tuna in olive oil, drained
1 tbsp capers, drained
1 tbsp parsley, chopped

Mixed Pepper Tuna Linguine

324

Add a quarter of each colour pepper (making 1 whole) to add more colour to this dish.

325

SERVES 4

Gnocchi with Pesto

PREPARATION TIME: 1 HOUR

COOKING TIME: 5 MINUTES

INGREDIENTS

700 g floury potatoes, such as Maris Piper, peeled
250 g plain (all purpose) flour
1 egg, beaten
Nutmeg, grated to taste
2 handfuls pine nuts, lightly toasted
1 clove of garlic, peeled and chopped
2 bunches basil
80 g / 3 oz / ⅓ cup Parmesan, grated
Olive oil

- Boil the potatoes in boiling salted water for 25 minutes.
- Drain and mash thoroughly until completely smooth. Leave to cool. Tip the cooled potatoes into a bowl and work in the flour, egg, a pinch of salt and nutmeg until you have a smooth dough.
- Cut the dough in half and roll out into sausage shapes. Cut into pieces 3 cm long and press down gently with a fork to make the indentations. Place on a floured baking sheet to cook when ready.
- Combine the pine nuts, garlic and basil with the Parmesan in a food processor to a rough paste. Drizzle in enough oil to make a loose sauce. Season carefully.
- To cook the gnocchi, bring a large pan of salted water to the boil then add the gnocchi. When they float to the top, they are ready, so remove and drain on kitchen paper.
- Toss with the pesto and serve.

Gnocchi with Sun-dried Tomatoes

326

Alternatively add a handful sun-dried tomatoes instead of the basil to the pesto.

327

SERVES 4

Trines with Cherry Tomatoes

PREPARATION TIME: 5 MINUTES

COOKING TIME: 10-15 MINUTES

INGREDIENTS

500 g / 1 lb / 2 cups trine pasta or any other crinkle-edged shape
2 tbsp olive oil
2 cloves garlic, finely sliced
300 g / 10 oz / 1 ¼ cups cherry tomatoes
1 tbsp balsamic vinegar

- Cook the pasta in boiling salted water according to packet instructions.
- Drain, reserving a little cooking water and keep warm.
- Meanwhile heat the oil in a pan and gently fry the garlic.
- Add the tomatoes and a little seasoning and cook until soft.
- Toss with the drained pasta, 2 tbsp water, some seasoning and the balsamic and serve.

Farfalle with Cherry Tomatoes

328

Using this bitesize pasta creates a different textured dish, use the same weight and cook the same.

329

SERVES 4

Farfalle and Sun-dried Tomato Salad

- Cook the pasta in boiling salted water according to packet instructions. Drain, toss with a little oil and keep warm.
- Meanwhile heat the oil in a pan and gently fry the garlic.
- Add the tomatoes and capers and warm through.
- Toss with the cooked pasta and stir through the parsley and season with salt and pepper.

PREPARATION TIME: 5 MINUTES

COOKING TIME: 12 MINUTES

INGREDIENTS

500 g / 1 lb / 2 cups farfalle pasta
4 tbsp olive oil
1 clove garlic, finely chopped
185 g / 6 ½ oz / 2 / 3 cup sundried tomatoes, drained and chopped
1 tbsp capers, drained
1 tbsp flat leaf parsley, chopped

Farfalle and Olive Salad

330

Mix 185 g / 6 ½ oz / ⅔ cups chopped Green and Black Olives to this to dish for olive lovers.

331

SERVES 4

Tagliatelle with Courgette, Ham and Goat's Cheese

- Cook the pasta in boiling salted water according to packet instructions. Drain and toss with a little oil.
- Meanwhile thinly slice the courgettes lengthways with a vegetable peeler to make ribbons.
- Saute the courgette for 2 minutes in a little olive oil.
- Toss the pasta with the courgettes, ham, cheese and olive oil, then season and serve.

PREPARATION TIME: 10 MINUTES

COOKING TIME: 12 MINUTES

INGREDIENTS

500 g / 1 lb / 2 cups tagliatelle
2 small courgettes (zucchini)
4 slices English-style ham, chopped
150 g crottin de Chavignol goat's cheese, crumbled
2tbsp olive oil

Spicy Tagliatelle with Courgette

332

Add a little finely chopped red chilli for a kick

333

SERVES 4

Tortelloni with Spinach Puree and Ham

PREPARATION TIME: 10 MINUTES

COOKING TIME: 20 MINUTES

....

INGREDIENTS

500 g / 1lb / 2 cups ready made
spinach and ricotta tortelloni
4 slices air-dried ham
1 tbsp butter
2 shallots, finely chopped
200 g / 6 ½ oz / ¾ cup spinach
100 ml / 3 ½ fl. oz / ½ cup chicken
stock
4 tbsp single (light) cream

- Cook the pasta in boiling salted water according to packet instructions.
- Drain and toss with a little butter and keep warm.
- Meanwhile heat the butter in a pan and add the shallots and spinach, stirring until the spinach has wilted.
- Tip into a food processor and add a thestock. Blend until smooth, adding the cream. Season with salt and pepper and reheat gently.
- Tear the ham into pieces.
- Spoon the puree onto a plate and top with the pasta. Decorate with the pieces of ham.

Tortelloni with Bechamel Puree   **334**

If preferred make a béchamel sauce (P X) and stir the puree into that. Toss with the pasta and bake in a hot oven for 15 minutes or so until bubbling.

335

SERVES 4

Ravioli with Herbs

PREPARATION TIME: 1 HOUR

COOKING TIME: 5 MINUTES

....

INGREDIENTS

500 g / 1lb / 2 cups (see p.) rolled into
2 sheets

FOR THE FILLING:
2 tbsp basil, chopped
200 g / 6 ½ oz / ¾ cup ricotta
3 tbsp olive oil
4 tbsp parsley, chopped
2 tbsp chives, chopped
2 tbsp butter

- Stir the basil into the ricotta with a little oil, parsley and seasoning.
- Lay a sheet of pasta onto a floured work surface and place teaspoonfuls of the mixture at intervals along the sheet, leaving a 5cm / 2" gap between each mound. Brush around each mound with a little beaten egg.
- Top with the second sheet of pasta and press down lightly around each mound, pressing out all the air. Cut out or stamp out with a cutter and lay on a baking tray.
- Repeat and then cover the ravioli with a damp tea towel until ready to cook.
- Cook the ravioli in boiling salted water for 2 minutes, removing with a slotted spoon and drain on kitchen paper.
- Heat the butter in a pan until foaming then pour over the ravioli. Decorate with chives.

Tomato Ravioli with Herbs   **336**

Add 2 halved tomatoes (roasted for 15 minutes) to this dish.

337

SERVES 4

Farfalle with Courgette Saffron Sauce

Farfelle with Spicy Courgette

338

Add 1 red chilli finely chopped with the courgettes (zucchini) for a fiery flavour.

Farfelle with Ham

339

Meat lovers could add a little chopped ham or chicken with the courgettes (zucchini).

Farfelle with Aubergine

340

Replace the courgette with aubergine and cook the same.

PREPARATION TIME: 10 MINUTES

COOKING TIME: 15 MINUTES

INGREDIENTS

500 g / 1 lb / 2 cups farfalle
2 courgettes (zucchini), grated
2 tbsp butter, or olive oil
1 clove garlic, finely chopped
Pinch saffron
75 ml / 3 fl. oz / ⅓ cup chicken stock
Handful thyme leaves
½ lemon, grated zest

- Cook the pasta in boiling salted water according to packet instructions.
- Meanwhile cook the courgettes (zucchini) in butter or oil with the garlic until softened.
- Add the saffron to the stock and add to the sauce. Add the thyme leaves and reduce until the stock is syrupy.
- Add the zest and season.
- Toss the drained pasta with the sauce and serve.

341

SERVES 6

Spaghetti and Meatballs

PREPARATION TIME: 50 MINUTES

COOKING TIME: 30 MINUTES

INGREDIENTS

400 g / 13 ½ oz / 1 ½ cups minced beef
1 egg
2 tbsp parsley, chopped
1 thick slice of white bread, crusts removed soaked in 2 tbsp milk
3 tbsp olive oil
300 ml / 10 fl. oz / 1 ¼ cups passata
400 ml / 13 ½ fl. oz / 1 ½ cups beef stock
1 tsp sugar
350 g / 12 oz / 1 ⅓ cups spaghetti
2 tbsp Parmesan, grated to serve

- Place the meat in a large bowl with the egg and 1 tbsp parsley and season.
- Mulch the bread in your fingers and crumble into the mix.
- Mix everything together with your hands to become smooth and sticky.
- Roll into small walnut-sized balls with cold wet hands, place on a tray and chill for 30 minutes.
- Heat the oil in a pan and fry the meatballs in batches.
- Add the passata and stock, then add the sugar and season and bring to the boil. Lower the heat and simmer for about 20 minutes.
- Meanwhile cook the pasta in boiling salted water according to packet instructions.
- Drain and tip into a large bowl.
- Pour the sauce over the pasta, sprinkle over the parsley and Parmesan and serve.

Spaghetti with Pork Meatballs   **342**

Use minced pork for a milder taste and make larger meatballs to serve 4 people.

343

SERVES 4

Spaghetti alla Vongole

PREPARATION TIME: 10 MINUTES

COOKING TIME: 15 MINUTES

INGREDIENTS

500 g / 1 lb / 2 cups spaghetti
1 tbsp olive oil
1 shallot, finely chopped
2 cloves garlic, finely chopped
1 red chilli, finely chopped
500 g / 1 lb / 2 cups clams, cleaned
120 ml / 4 fl. oz / ½ cup dry white wine
1 tbsp parsley, chopped
½ lemon, juiced

- Cook the spaghetti in boiling salted water according to packet instructions.
- Meanwhile heat the oil in a large pan and sweat the shallot, garlic and chilli until soft.
- Add the clams and white wine, cover with a lid and leave to cook for 5-6 minutes until the clams have opened.
- Drain the pasta and reserve a little of the cooking water.
- Carefully drain the clams into a colander over a bowl, discarding the sand collected at the bottom.
- Return the clams and their cooking liquor, the pasta and 2 tbsp water to the pan with the parsley and lemon juice. Season and reheat gently.
- Serve immediately.

Spaghetti with Mussels   **344**

Use mussels for a slightly richer seafood taste.

345

SERVES 4

Penne with Roasted Vegetables

Penne with Roasted Chilli Vegetables

346

Add 1 chopped chilli to the vegetables for a spicy kick.

Pepper Penne

347

Add a bunch of rocket (arugua), chopped, for peppery flavour

Southern Mediterranean Fusilli

348

Swap the weight of penne for the same weight of fusilli.

PREPARATION TIME: 10 MINUTES

COOKING TIME: 30 MINUTES

INGREDIENTS

1 aubergine (eggplant), chopped
1 courgette, (zucchini) chopped
300 g / 10 oz / 1 ¼ cups cherry tomatoes
1 red pepper, deseeded and chopped
1 yellow pepper, deseeded and chopped
1 tbsp olive oil
500 g / 1 lb / 2 cups penne pasta
2 tbsp Parmesan, grated
1 tbsp basil, chopped

- Preheat the oven to 200°C / 400F / gas 6.
- Place all the vegetables in a roasting tin and toss with oil and seasoning. Roast in the oven for about 25-30 minutes until tender and starting to blacken slightly.
- Meanwhile cook the penne in boiling salted water according to packet instructions. Drain and keep warm.
- When the vegetables are cooked, tip with all their juices into a pan and add the pasta. Toss thoroughly.
- Serve with Parmesan and basil leaves.

349

SERVES 4

Neopolitan Casareccia Salad

Spicy Neopolitan Casareccia Salad

350

Add pinch dried chilli flakes for heat

Casareccia Salad with Herbs

351

Use a mixture of herbs such as oregano and basil for a herbier dish.

Neopolitan Casareccia Shrimp Salad

352

Add 250 g / 8 oz of shrimp to this dish when tossing the pasta with the cooked vegetables.

PREPARATION TIME: 10 MINUTES

COOKING TIME: 12 MINUTES

INGREDIENTS

300 g / 10 oz / 1 ¼ cups cherry tomatoes, halved
2 handfuls black olives, chopped
3 tbsp capers, drained
2 tbsp olive oil
500 g / 1 lb / 2 cups casareccia or other shaped pasta
1 tbsp basil, chopped

- Toss the tomatoes, olives and capers with oil and seasoning and leave to macerate.
- Cook the pasta in boiling salted water according to packet instructions. Drain.
- Toss the pasta with the macerated vegetables and basil, adding more oil and seasoning if necessary.
- Serve warm.

353

SERVES 4

Tagliatelle with Duck Foie Gras

- Heat a frying pan until very hot and sear the pate on each side until golden.
- Cook through for another minute then remove to a plate.
- Cook the pasta in boiling salted water according to packet instructions.
- Drain and toss with the butter and basil.
- Cut the pate into cubes and toss quickly with the pasta, salt and pepper. Serve immediately.

PREPARATION TIME: 5 MINUTES

COOKING TIME: 5-8 MINUTES

INGREDIENTS

500 g / 1 lb / 2 cups fresh tagliatelle
2 tbsp butter
4 slices duck liver pate
2 tbsp basil, chopped

Taglitelle with Tomato   354

Add 2 chopped tomatoes for freshness.

355

SERVES 4

Pesto Gnocchi with Broad Beans

- Boil the potatoes in boiling salted water for 25 minutes. Drain and mash thoroughly, until completely smooth. Leave to cool.
- Tip the cooled potatoes into a bowl and work in the flour, egg, a pinch of salt and nutmeg until you have a smooth dough. Cut the dough in half and roll out to make 2 fat sausages.
- Cut into pieces about 3cm long and press down gently with a fork. Place on a floured baking sheet to cook.
- Cook the broad beans in boiling water for 3-5 minutes.
- Once tender, drain and refresh under cold water. Pod them out of the grey skins.
- To cook the gnocchi, bring a large pan of salted water to the boil then add the gnocchi. When they float to the top, remove and drain on kitchen paper.
- Warm the pesto with the butter and toss with the beans and gnocchi. Scatter over Parmesan and serve.

PREPARATION TIME: 1 HOUR

COOKING TIME: 10 MINUTES

INGREDIENTS

700 g / 1 lb 8 oz potatoes
250 g / 9 oz / 2 ¼ cups plain
(all-purpose) flour
1 egg, beaten
salt
nutmeg
100 g / 3 ½ oz / ½ cup broad beans,
podded
3 tbsp pesto
1 tbsp butter
Parmesan, grated to serve

Pesto Gnocchi with Flageolet Beans   356

Instead of broad beans, use drained flageolet beans as a substitute.

103

SERVES 3-4

Chorizo Pizza

PREPARATION TIME 10 MINUTES

COOKING TIME 45 MINUTES

....

INGREDIENTS

500 g / 1 lb pizza dough (page 110)

FOR THE TOPPING, PER PIZZA:

6 tbsp tomato passata
6 slices chorizo sausage
6 roasted red peppers, torn
½ ball mozzarella, sliced
basil leaves
extra virgin olive oil
black pepper

- To make the pizza dough, see page 110.
- Flour the dough, cover with film and leave to rest for 30 minutes.
- Roll the pizzas out about 30 minutes before you want to cook them. Preheat the oven to 250°C (230° fan) / 500F / gas 9. Flour the surface, tear off a piece of dough and roll into a rough circle about 0.5 cm thick.
- Dust each one with a little flour and lay out on the surface.
- Spread the base of each pizza with the tomato passata, then with the cheese, peppers and chorizo.
- Place either directly on the bars of the oven or on a preheated baking sheet for 8-10 minutes until golden and crisp.
- Drizzle with extra virgin olive oil, grind over some pepper, scatter with basil and serve hot.

Salami and Sausage Pizza

Use salami slices and frankfurter slices instead of chorizo.

SERVES 3-4

Pepperoni and Mozzarella Pizza

PREPARATION TIME:
45 MINUTES + PROVING TIME

COOKING TIME: 8-10 MINUTES

....

INGREDIENTS

500 g / 1 lb pizza dough (page 110)

FOR THE TOPPING: PER PIZZA

6 tbsp tomato passata
6-8 slices pepperoni
¼ red onion, finely sliced
½ ball mozzarella, sliced
rocket leaves
extra virgin olive oil

- To make the pizza dough, see page 110.
- Roll the pizzas out about 30 minutes before you want to cook them. Preheat the oven to 250°C (230° fan) / 500F / gas 9. Flour the surface; tear off a piece of dough and roll into a rough circle about 0.5 cm thick.
- Dust each one with a little flour and lay out on the surface.
- Spread the base of each pizza with the tomato passata, then with the ingredients, then cover the whole with mozzarella cheese.
- Place either directly on the bars of the oven or on a preheated baking sheet for 8-10 minutes until golden and crisp.
- Drizzle with extra virgin olive oil and serve hot.

Chorizo and Mozzarella Pizza

Use chorizo slices instead of pepperoni.

360

361

SERVES 3-4 Cheese and Rocket Pizza

- To make the pizza dough, see page 110.
- Flour the dough, cover with film and leave to rest for 30 minutes.
- Roll the pizzas out 30 minutes before you want to cook them. Preheat the oven to 250°C (230° fan) / 500F / gas 9. Flour the surface; tear off a piece of dough and roll into a rough circle about 0.5 cm thick.
- Dust each one with a little flour and lay out on the surface.
- Spread the base of each pizza with the tomato passata, then with the cheeses and rocket.
- Place either directly on the bars of the oven or on a preheated baking sheet for 8-10 minutes until golden and crisp.
- Drizzle with extra virgin olive oil, grind over some pepper and serve hot.

PREPARATION TIME:
45 MINUTES + PROVING TIME
COOKING TIME: 8-10 MINUTES
....

INGREDIENTS

500 g / 1 lb pizza dough (page 110)
FOR THE TOPPING, PER PIZZA:
6 tbsp tomato passata
50 g / 2 oz mozzarella, sliced
50 g / 2 oz Gorgonzola, sliced
50 g / 2 oz Taleggio, sliced
small handful rocket leaves
extra virgin olive oil
black pepper

Cheese and Sage Pizza   362

Swap the rocket leaves for sage leaves making a less peppery pizza.

363

SERVES 3-4 Ham, Onion and Emmental Pizza

- To make the pizza dough, see page 110.
- Flour the dough, cover with film and leave to rest for 30 minutes.
- Roll the pizzas out about 30 minutes before you want to cook them. Preheat the oven to 250°C (230° fan) / 500F / gas 9. Flour the surface, tear off a piece of dough and roll into a rough circle about 0.5 cm thick.
- Dust each one with a little flour and lay out on the surface.
- Spread the base of each pizza with the passata, then with the ham, onion and cheese
- Place either directly on the bars of the oven or on a preheated baking sheet for 8-10 minutes until golden and crisp.
- Drizzle with extra virgin olive oil, grind over some pepper, scatter with basil and serve hot.

PREPARATION TIME:
45 MINUTES + PROVING TIME
COOKING TIME: 8-10 MINUTES
....

INGREDIENTS

500 g / 1 lb pizza dough (page 110)
FOR THE TOPPING: PER PIZZA
6 tbsp passata
6 slices ham
½ red or white onion, finely sliced
100 g / 3 ½ oz / ½ cup Emmental, sliced
basil leaves
extra virgin olive oil
black pepper

Prosciutto, Onion and Emmental Pizza   364

Change the weight of hame for prosciutto for a more authentic Italian dish.

365

SERVES 4-6

Salami and Ricotta Pie

Ricotta and Courgette Pie

366

Use 1 courgette, grated and folded into the ricotta.

Chorizo and Ricotta Pie

367

Replace the salami slices with chorizo chunks.

Salami and Red Pepper

368

Half the weight of the cherry tomatoes and replace with red peppers to give the dish a crunch.

PREPARATION TIME:
40 MINUTES + PROVING TIME

COOKING TIME: 45 MINUTES

....

INGREDIENTS

500 g / 1 lb pizza dough (page 110)
5 eggs, separated
300 g / 10 oz / 1 ¼ cups ricotta
1 ball mozzarella, diced
100 g salami, chopped
5 tbsp Parmesan, grated
100 g / 3 ½ oz / ½ cup cherry
tomatoes, halved
salt and pepper

- To make the pizza dough, see page 110.
- Preheat the oven to 180°C (160° fan) / 350F / gas 5.
- Beat 4 of the egg yolks together and then beat into the ricotta. Season well.
- Whisk all the egg whites to stiff peaks and then fold into the ricotta mixture.
- Fold in the mozzarella, salami and Parmesan.
- Punch the air out of the pizza dough and roll ⅔ of it into a 35 cm circle.
- Line a greased pizza or pie pan with it, draping the extra dough over the edge.
- Spoon the filling in. Top with the cherry tomatoes
- Roll the remaining dough out thinly and lay over the top of the filling.
- Press the edges down lightly to seal and trim off any excess.
- Whisk the remaining egg yolk and brush over the pastry.
- Bake in the oven for about 45 minutes until golden.
- Leave to stand for 10 minutes before serving.

369

SERVES 4

Tomato and Mozzarella Pizza

- To make the pizza dough, see page 110.
- Flour the dough, cover with film and leave to rest for 30 minutes.
- Roll the pizzas out 30 minutes before you want to cook them. Preheat the oven to 250°C / 500F / gas 9. Flour the surface, tear off a piece of dough and roll into a rough circle about 0.5cm thick.
- Dust each one with a little flour and lay out on the surface.
- Spread the base of each pizza with the tomato passata, then with tomatoes. Scatter over the garlic and oregano, then lay over the mozzarella.
- Place either directly on the bars of the oven or on a preheated baking sheet for 8-10 minutes until golden and crisp.
- Drizzle with extra virgin olive oil, grind over some pepper and serve hot.

PREPARATION TIME:
45 MINUTES + PROVING TIME

COOKING TIME: 8-10 MINUTES

INGREDIENTS

500 g / 1 lb pizza dough (page 110)

FOR THE TOPPING, PER PIZZA:
6 tbsp tomato passata
150 g / 5 oz / ⅔ cup cherry tomatoes, halved
1 clove of garlic, finely chopped
½ ball mozzarella, sliced
1 tsp dried oregano
extra virgin olive oil
black pepper

Tomato and Fontina Pizza

370

Use fontina, a good melting cheese, instead of mozzarella.

371

SERVES 4

Pear, Spinach and Gorgonzola Pizza

- To make the pizza dough, see page 110. Flour the dough, cover with film and leave to rest for 30 minutes. Place the spinach in a pan with a tbsp of water, cover with a lid and cook over a low heat until wilted.
- Drain the spinach through a sieve, pushing hard with a wooden spoon to extract as much moisture as possible.
- Roll the pizzas out 30 minutes before you want to cook them. Preheat the oven to 250°C / 500F / gas 9.
- Flour the surface, tear off a piece of dough and roll into a circle about 0.5cm / ⅕" thick. Dust each one with a little flour and lay out on the surface.
- Spread the base of each pizza with the spinach, then top with pear and Gorgonzola. Bake for 8-10 minutes.
- Drizzle with olive oil, grind over some pepper, scatter over the pine nuts and rocket and serve hot.

PREPARATION TIME: 1 HOUR

COOKING TIME: 8-10 MINUTES

INGREDIENTS

500 g / 1 lb pizza dough (page 110)

FOR THE TOPPING
(Per pizza)
200 g / 6 ½ oz / ¾ cup spinach leaves
1 pear, cored and sliced
100 g / 3 ½ oz / ½ cup Gorgonzola, sliced
1 tbsp Olive oil
1 tbsp pine nuts, lightly toasted
Small handful rocket (arugula) leaves

Parma Ham and Pear Pizza

372

Add 2 slices of Parma ham to each pizza before adding the Gorgonzola

Pear and Watercress Pizza

373

Wilt a handful of chopped watercress with the spinach for extra peppery bite

374

MAKES 2

Cherry Tomato Focaccia

PREPARATION TIME: 40 MINUTES
+ 2 HOURS PROVING TIME

COOKING TIME: 20 MINUTES

INGREDIENTS

750 g / 1 ¼ lb / 3 cups grade '00' flour
½ tsp salt
2 tsp fast-action dried yeast
150 ml / 5 fl. oz / ⅔ cup extra virgin olive oil
450 ml / 1 pint / 2 cups lukewarm water
coarse sea salt
150 g cherry tomatoes
bunch of rosemary leaves

- Sift the flour and salt into a bowl and make a well in the centre. Pour 50 ml of the oil into the flour, add the yeast and rub together with your fingers until it resembles breadcrumbs.
- Pour in the water and mix until the dough comes together. Tip the dough onto a floured surface and knead for 10 minutes. Place in a lightly oiled bowl, cover with film and leave to rise in a warm place until doubled in size, about 1 ½ hours.
- Take the dough out of the bowl, punch out the air and divide into 2 balls. Roll out 2 circles and place in 2 oiled pizza pans. Cover and leave to rise for 30 minutes.
- Preheat the oven to 200° C (180° fan) / 400F / gas 6.
- Uncover the dough and push your fingertips in all over to make dimples. Drizzle with oil so the dimples fill up. Top with tomatoes and rosemary. Sprinkle with salt.
- Spray with water and bake for 20 minutes. Transfer to a wire rack to cool before serving.

Tuna and Tomato Focaccia

375

Use 60 g / 2 oz canned tuna as an additional topping.

376

SERVES 3-4

Pizza Pancetta

PREPARATION TIME: 45 MINUTES
+ PROVING TIME

COOKING TIME: 8-10 MINUTES

INGREDIENTS

500 g / 1 lb pizza dough (page 110)
FOR THE TOPPING, PER PIZZA:
6 tbsp tomato passata
2-3 slices pancetta
1 tbsp rosemary leaves, finely chopped
½ onion, peeled and finely sliced
extra virgin olive oil
black pepper

- To make the pizza dough, see page 110.
- Flour the dough, cover with film and leave to rest for 30 minutes.
- Roll the pizzas out about 30 minutes before you want to cook them. Preheat the oven to 250°C (230° fan) / 500F / gas 9. Flour the surface, tear off a piece of dough and roll into a rough circle about 0.5 cm thick.
- Dust each one with a little flour and lay out on the surface.
- Spread the base of each pizza with the tomato passata, then with the pancetta, rosemary and onion.
- Place either directly on the bars of the oven or on a preheated baking sheet for 8-10 minutes until golden and crisp.
- Drizzle with extra virgin olive oil, grind over some pepper and serve hot.

Sweetcorn and Pancetta Pizza

377

Add 2 tbsp tinned, drained sweetcorn.

378

SERVES 3-4

Pesto, Pepper and Olive Pizza

- To make the pizza dough, see page 110.
- Flour the dough, cover with film and leave to rest for 30 minutes.
- Roll the pizzas out about 30 minutes before you want to cook them. Preheat the oven to 250°C (230° fan) / 500F / gas 9. Flour the surface, tear off a piece of dough and roll into a rough circle about 0.5 cm thick.
- Dust each one with a little flour and lay out on the surface.
- Spread the base of each pizza with the pesto, then with the peppers, olives and mozzarella.
- Place either directly on the bars of the oven or on a preheated baking sheet for 8-10 minutes until golden and crisp.
- Drizzle with extra virgin olive oil, grind over some pepper and serve hot.

Potato and Pesto Pizza

379

Dice and roast a small potato and add it to the topping of each pizza.

PREPARATION TIME:
45 MINUTES + PROVING TIME
COOKING TIME: 8-10 MINUTES

INGREDIENTS

500 g / 1 lb pizza dough (page 110)
FOR THE TOPPING, PER PIZZA:
2 tbsp pesto
2 tbsp roasted peppers, from a jar
small handful black olives, stoned
½ ball mozzarella, sliced
extra virgin olive oil
black pepper

380

SERVES 3-4

Pizza Bolognese

- To make the pizza dough, see page 110.
- Flour the dough, cover with film and leave to rest for 30 minutes. Heat the olive oil in a pan and dry the onion and garlic until soft and translucent.
- Turn up the heat and fry the meat briskly until brown. Stir in the passata and oregano, season and simmer for 20 minutes until the sauce thickenS. Set aside to cool.
- Roll the pizzas out about 30 minutes before you want to cook them. Preheat the oven to 250°C (230° fan) / 500F / gas 9. Flour the surface, tear off a piece of dough and roll into a rough circle about 0.5 cm thick.
- Dust each one with a little flour and lay out on the surface. Spread the base of each pizza with the Bolognese sauce, then top with slices of mozzarella.
- Place on a preheated baking sheet for 8-10 minutes until golden. Drizzle with extra virgin olive oil, grind over some pepper and serve hot.

Lamb Pizza Bolognese

381

Replace the minced beef with 450 g / 1 lb / 2 cups of minced lamb.

PREPARATION TIME:
45 MINUTES + PROVING TIME
COOKING TIME: 40 MINUTES

INGREDIENTS

500 g / 1 lb pizza dough (page 110)
FOR THE TOPPING:
1 tbsp olive oil
1 onion, peeled and finely chopped
2 cloves of garlic, finely chopped
450 g / 1 lb / 2 cups minced beef
400 ml / 13 ½ fl. oz / 1 ½ cups passata
2 tsp dried oregano
2 balls mozzarella
extra virgin olive oil
black pepper

382

SERVES 2

Ham and Cheese Calzone

Ham and Tomato Calzone

383

Add 2 chopped tomatoes into the filling.

Mushroom and Cheese Calzone

384

Use sliced cooked mushrooms instead of the ham for a vegetarian option.

Cheese and Tomato Calzone

385

Rather than add ham add 2 tomatoes sliced as a vegetarian option.

PREPARATION TIME:
45 MINUTES + PROVING TIME

COOKING TIME: 35 MINUTES

....

INGREDIENTS

500 g / 1 lb pizza dough (page 110)
FOR THE TOPPING:
1 ball fresh mozzarella
1 tbsp fresh rosemary leaves, finely chopped
1 clove of garlic, finely chopped
4 slices Parma ham
salt and pepper
extra virgin olive oil

- To make the dough, pour the flours and salt into a bowl and make a well in the centre, add the yeast and sugar to the water, mix with a fork and leave for a few minutes.
- Bring in all the flour, working your way towards the outer edges, mixing well. When it starts to come together, use your hands and pat it into a ball.
- Knead the dough for around 10 minutes until the dough is smooth and elastic.
- Flour the dough, cover with film and leave to rest for 30 minutes. Roll the dough out about 30 minutes before you want to cook it. Preheat the oven to 250°C (230° fan) / 500F / gas 9.
- Lightly squeeze any excess moisture out of the mozzarella. Tear the ham into pieces.
- Cut the dough in half and pull or roll out into 2 x 25 cm circles and slide onto baking parchment. Place on a baking sheet.
- Cover one half of each circle with the filling, leaving about 1 cm around the edge to seal. Season.
- Fold the uncovered half over the filling and pinch and twist the edges firmly together to seal.
- Bake for 10 minutes and then slide out the baking parchment. Cook for a further 25 minutes or until puffed and golden.
- Drizzle with a little oil and stand for 2 minutes before serving.

Spring Vegetable Panzerotti

SERVES 4

386

- To make the pizza dough, see page 110.
- Heat the olive oil in a pan and cook the grated courgette gently for about 8 minutes until soft. Season and set aside to cool.
- Uncover the dough, punch out the air and pull out, using your hands, until it is very thin. Cut out about 15 circles with a cutter or even an upturned cup.
- Place spoonfuls of the courgette onto one half of the pastry circle. Add the cubed mozzarella, zest and chilli if using. Fold the other half over, pinching to seal. Use the tines of a fork to make the decorative.
- Heat the oil to 190°C (170° fan) / 375F. Deep-fry the panzerotti in batches until puffed and golden.

PREPARATION TIME:
45 MINUTES + PROVING TIME

COOKING TIME: 5 MINUTES

INGREDIENTS

FOR THE DOUGH:
200 g / 6 ½ oz / ¾ cup strong white bread flour
50 g / 1 ½ oz semolina flour
¼ tbsp salt
½ x 7g sachet of dried yeast
¼ tbsp caster (superfine) sugar
175 ml / ¼ pint / ¾ cup lukewarm water

FOR THE FILLING:
2 tbsp olive oil
2 courgettes, grated
100 g / 3 ½ oz / ½ cup mozzarella, cubed
zest of ½ lemon
1 red chilli, finely diced, optional
vegetable oil, for deep frying

Asparagus Frittata

SERVES 6

387

- Preheat the oven to 180°C (160° fan) / 350F / gas 5.
- Beat the eggs and the crème fraiche in a large bowl.
- Snap the woody ends off the asparagus and discard. Cut the asparagus into short lengths.
- Fry the onion gently in 2 tbsp olive oil until deep gold and soft – about 20 minutes
- Pour the egg mixture in, add the asparagus and distribute evenly.
- Bake for about 35 minutes until puffed and golden.
- The egg should be cooked through.
- Cut into squares and serve warm or cold

PREPARATION TIME: 30 MINUTES

COOKING TIME: 55 MINUTES

INGREDIENTS

8 eggs
1 tbsp crème fraiche
1 bunch asparagus
1 onion, peeled and thickly sliced
olive oil
salt and pepper

Courgette Frittata

388

Substitute 2 diced courgettes for the asparagus and fry them with the onion before adding the egg.

389
SERVES 4

Tomato Risotto

PREPARATION TIME: 10 MINUTES

COOKING TIME: 25 MINUTES

INGREDIENTS

2 tbsp olive oil
40 g / 1 oz butter
1 onion, peeled and finely chopped
2 cloves of garlic, finely chopped
4 ripe tomatoes, chopped
1 tbsp sun-blush tomatoes, finely sliced
320 g / 11 oz / 1 ⅓ cups risotto rice
100 ml / 3 ½ fl. oz / ½ cup dry white wine
4 tbsp tomato passata
1 l / 2 ¼ pints / 4 ¼ cups chicken or vegetable stock

salt and pepper
3 tbsp butter
120 g / 4 oz / ½ cup Parmesan, grated
1 bunch basil leaves

- Heat the oil and butter in a large pan and add the onion and garlic. Cook until soft.
- Add the fresh and preserved tomatoes to the pan.
- Add the rice and stir to coat in the butter.
- Pour in the wine and stir the rice while the wine is absorbed, then stir in the tomato passata.
- Reduce the heat a little and add the stock, a ladleful at a time, stirring continuously.
- Keep stirring in the stock and tasting the rice. After about 15-20 minutes the rice should be soft but with a slight bite. If you've run out of stock before the rice is cooked, simply use water.
- Season and remove from the heat. Add the butter and Parmesan and leave to melt into the risotto.
- Stir through the basil and serve immediately.

Tomato and Mascarpone Risotto

390

For a creamier risotto, stir in 60 g mascarpone at the end.

391
SERVES 4

Rustic Tomato Soup

PREPARATION TIME 15 MINUTES

COOKING TIME 40 MINUTES

INGREDIENTS

2 tbsp olive oil
1 onion, peeled and chopped
1 carrot, peeled and finely chopped
1 celery stalk, finely chopped
2 cloves of garlic, chopped
1 courgette, finely chopped
2 potatoes, peeled and finely chopped
2 slices Parma ham, chopped
1 x 400 g can chopped tomatoes
1 dried red chilli, chopped
1 l / 2 ¼ pints / 4 ¼ cups chicken stock
salt and pepper
extra virgin olive oil

- Heat the oil in a pan and sweat the onion, carrot and celery without colouring.
- Add the garlic and cook for 2 minutes until soft.
- Add the courgettes and potatoes, stir well and leave to soften for a 5-10 minutes, then add the ham.
- Pour in the tomatoes, crumble in a little of the chilli, then stir in the stock.
- Bring to a simmer and leave to cook until the vegetables are tender – about 20 minutes.
- Taste and adjust the seasoning if necessary, adding chilli if desired.
- Roughly mash the vegetables with a potato masher or pulse in a liquidiser.
- Serve drizzled with olive oil.

Chicken and Pepper Risotto

392

SERVES 4

Chicken, Mushroom and Pepper Risotto

393

Add 100 g sliced button mushrooms with the chicken and peppers.

Chicken and Onion Risotto

394

Swap the pepper for an additional 1 onion sliced for crunch and cook the same.

Chilli Chicken Risotto

395

When frying the chicken sprinkle a few chilli flakes for a spicier risotto.

PREPARATION TIME: 15 MINUTES

COOKING TIME: 35 MINUTES

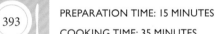

INGREDIENTS

2 tbsp olive oil
40 g / 1 oz butter
1 onion, peeled and finely chopped
2 cloves of garlic, finely chopped
2 chicken breasts, skinned and cubed
1 red pepper, deseeded and chopped
1 yellow pepper, deseeded and chopped
1 red chilli, deseeded if preferred and finely chopped
320 g / 11 oz / 1 ⅓ cups risotto rice
100 ml / 3 ½ fl. oz / ½ cup dry white wine
1 l / 2 ¼ pints / 4 ¼ cups chicken or vegetable stock

salt and pepper
3 tbsp butter
120 g / 4 oz / ½ cup Parmesan, grated

- Heat the oil and butter in a large pan and add the onion and garlic. Cook until soft.
- Add the chicken and peppers to the pan. Cook for 10 minutes or until softened.
- Add the chilli and stir through. Add the rice and stir to coat in the butter.
- Pour in the wine and stir the rice while the wine is absorbed.
- Reduce the heat a little and add the hot stock, a ladleful at a time, stirring continuously.
- Keep stirring in the stock and tasting the rice. After about 15-20 minutes the rice should be soft but with a slight bite. If you've run out of stock before the rice is cooked, simply use water.
- Season and remove from the heat. Add the butter and Parmesan and leave to melt into the risotto.
- Serve immediately.

396
SERVES 4

Chicken and Tomato Risotto

- Heat the oil and butter in a large pan and add the onion and garlic. Cook until soft.
- Add the chicken to the pan and cook until golden. Add the rice and stir to coat in the butter. Pour in the wine and stir the rice while the wine is absorbed.
- Reduce the heat a little and add the stock, a ladleful at a time, stirring continuously.
- Keep stirring in the stock and tasting the rice. After about 15-20 minutes the rice should be soft but with a slight bite. If you've run out of stock before the rice is cooked, simply use water.
- Towards the end of cooking, stir in the tomatoes, so they retain their shape and fresh flavour.
- Season and remove from the heat. Add the butter and Parmesan and leave to melt into the risotto.
- Stir in the basil and serve immediately.

PREPARATION TIME: 10 MINUTES

COOKING TIME: 25 MINUTES

INGREDIENTS

2 tbsp olive oil
40 g / 1 oz butter
1 onion, peeled and finely chopped
2 cloves of garlic, finely chopped
2 small chicken breasts, cubed
320 g / 11 oz / 1 ⅓ cups risotto rice
100 ml / 3 ½ fl. oz / ½ cup
white wine
1 l / 2 ¼ pints / 4 ¼ cups stock
handful cherry tomatoes, halved
3 tbsp butter
120 g / 4 oz / ½ cup Parmesan, grated
1 bunch basil leaves

397
SERVES 4

Beetroot Risotto

PREPARATION TIME: 15 MINUTES

COOKING TIME: 25 MINUTES

INGREDIENTS

2 tbsp olive oil
40 g / 1 oz butter
1 onion, peeled and finely chopped
2 cloves of garlic, finely chopped
1 tbsp thyme leaves

400 g / 13 ½ oz / 1 ½ cups beetroot, peeled and cubed
320 g / 11 oz / 1 ⅓ cups risotto rice
100 ml / 3 ½ fl. oz / ½ cup dry white wine
1 l / 2 ¼ pints / 4 ¼ cups stock
salt and pepper
3 tbsp butter
120 g / 4 oz / ½ cup goat's cheese
½ bunch flat leaf parsley, chopped

- Heat the oil and butter in a large pan and add the onion and garlic. Cook until soft and translucent.
- Add the beetroot to the pan. Cook for 5 minutes.
- Add the rice and stir to coat in the butter.
- Pour in the wine and stir the rice while the wine is absorbed.
- Reduce the heat a little and add the stock, a ladleful at a time, stirring continuously.
- Keep stirring in the stock and tasting the rice. After about 15-20 minutes the rice should be soft but with a slight bite. If you've run out of stock before the rice is cooked, simply use water.
- Season and remove from the heat. Add the butter and leave to melt into the risotto.
- Stir through the parsley and serve immediately with the goats cheese crumbled on top.

398
SERVES 4

Button Mushroom Risotto

PREPARATION TIME: 10 MINUTES

COOKING TIME: 25 MINUTES

INGREDIENTS

2 tbsp olive oil
40 g / 1 oz butter
1 onion, peeled and finely chopped
2 cloves of garlic, finely chopped
1 tbsp thyme leaves

200 g / 6 ½ oz / ¾ cup button mushrooms, sliced
320 g / 11 oz / 1 ⅓ cups risotto rice
100 ml / 3 ½ fl. oz / ½ cup white wine
1 l / 2 ¼ pints / 4 ¼ cups stock
salt and pepper
3 tbsp butter
120 g / 4 oz / ½ cup Parmesan, grated
½ bunch parsley, chopped
2-3 tbsp pesto
2 tbsp pine nuts, lightly toasted

- Heat the oil and butter in a large pan and add the onion and garlic. Cook until soft.
- Stir in the mushrooms and thyme and cook for a few minutes until the liquid evaporates.
- Add the rice and stir to coat in the butter.
- Pour in the wine and stir the rice while the wine is absorbed.
- Reduce the heat a little and add the hot stock, a ladleful at a time, stirring continuously.
- Keep stirring in the stock and tasting the rice. After about 15-20 minutes the rice should be soft but with a slight bite. If you've run out of stock before the rice is cooked, simply use water.
- Season and remove from the heat. Add the butter and Parmesan and leave to melt into the risotto.
- Stir through the parsley, pesto and pine nuts and serve.

399

SERVES 4

Ham and Pecorino Risotto

- Heat the oil and butter in a large pan and add the onion and garlic. Cook until soft.
- Add the pancetta and cook until golden.
- Add the rice and stir to coat in the butter.
- Pour in the wine and stir the rice while the wine is absorbed.
- Reduce the heat a little and add the stock, a ladleful at a time, stirring continuously.
- Keep stirring in the stock and tasting the rice. After about 15-20 minutes the rice should be soft but with a slight bite. If you've run out of stock before the rice is cooked, simply use water.
- Season and remove from the heat. Add the butter and pecorino and leave to melt into the risotto.
- Stir through the chopped Parma ham and parsley and serve immediately.

PREPARATION TIME: 5 MINUTES

COOKING TIME: 25 MINUTES

INGREDIENTS

2 tbsp olive oil
40 g / 1 oz butter
1 onion, peeled and finely chopped
100 g pancetta, cubed
320 g / 11 oz / 1 ⅓ cups risotto rice
100 ml / 3 ½ fl. oz / ½ cup dry white wine
1 l / 2 ¼ pints / 4 ¼ cups chicken or vegetable stock

salt and pepper
3 tbsp butter
120 g / 4 oz / ½ cup Pecorino, grated
4 slices Parma ham
½ bunch parsley, chopped

Ham and Gorgonzola Risotto

400

Substitute the Pecorino with Gorgonzola for a stronger cheese taste.

401

SERVES 4

Spicy Red Mullet Risotto

- Heat the stock and poach the fish for 10 minutes.
- Once cooked, keep the fish to one side in a warm place.
- Heat the oil and butter in a large pan and add the onion, garlic, chilli and smoked paprika. Cook until soft.
- Add the rice and stir to coat in the butter.
- Pour in the wine and stir the rice while the wine is absorbed.
- Reduce the heat a little and add the saffron and stock, a ladleful at a time, stirring continuously.
- Keep stirring in the stock and tasting the rice. After about 15-20 minutes the rice should be soft but with a slight bite. If you've run out of stock before the rice is cooked, simply use water.
- Season and remove from the heat. Add the butter and leave to melt into the risotto.
- Stir throughthe parsley, top with the fillets of mullet and serve immediately.

PREPARATION TIME: 20 MINUTES

COOKING TIME: 25 MINUTES

INGREDIENTS

1 l / 2 ¼ pints / 4 ¼ cups chicken stock
4 red mullet fillets, deboned
2 tbsp olive oil
40 g / 1 oz butter
1 onion, peeled and finely chopped
2 cloves of garlic, finely chopped
320 g / 11 oz / 1 ⅓ cups risotto rice
100 ml / 3 ½ fl. oz / ½ cup dry white wine
pinch saffron threads
1 red chilli, deseeded and finely chopped
½ tsp smoked paprika
salt and pepper
3 tbsp butter
½ bunch parsley, chopped

Red Mullet and Tomato Risotto

402

Stir in 2 ripe tomatoes, finely chopped towards the end of cooking.

403
SERVES 4

Tomato and Seafood Risotto

PREPARATION TIME: 10 MINUTES

COOKING TIME: 25 MINUTES

....

INGREDIENTS

2 tbsp olive oil
40 g / 1 oz / ⅕ cup butter
1 onion, peeled and finely chopped
2 cloves garlic, finely chopped
100 ml / 3 ½ fl. oz / ½ cup passata
320 g / 11 oz / 1 ⅓ cups risotto
(Arborio) rice
100 ml / 3 ½ fl. oz / ½ cup dry white
wine
1 l / 2 ¼ pints / 4 ¼ cups chicken or
vegetable stock
150 g / 5 oz hake fillet, skinned and
off the bone, cut into chunks
1 squid, cleaned and ink sac
removed, cut into squares
3 tbsp butter
1 lemon, grated zest and juiced
1 tbsp chervil, chopped
pinch dried chilli flakes
50 g / 3 tbsp Parmesan

- Heat the oil and butter in a large pan and add the onion and garlic. Cook until soft and translucent.
- Add the rice and stir to coat in the butter. Pour in the wine and stir the rice while the wine is absorbed.
- Once the wine has cooked in, reduce the heat a little and add the passata. Stir through then add the hot stock, a ladleful at a time, stirring fairly continuously.
- Half way through cooking add the hake and stir gently. After about 15-20 minutes the rice should be soft but with a slight bite.
- Season and remove from the heat. Add the butter and Parmesan and leave to melt into the risotto.
- Meanwhile heat a frying pan till very hot and sear the squid on all sides for 2-3 minutes or until just opaque.
- Stir in the lemon zest and juice, parsley and chilli. Season with salt and pepper.
- Serve the risotto immediately with the squid and Parmesan.

Tomato and Monkfish Risotto

404

Substitute the fish for any firm white fish or use prawns (shrimps) instead of squid – just add halfway through cooking with the fish.

405
SERVES 4

Prawn Risotto

PREPARATION TIME 5 MINUTES

COOKING TIME 25 MINUTES

....

INGREDIENTS

2 tbsp olive oil
40g / 1 oz / 1/5 cup butter
1 onion, peeled and finely chopped
2 cloves garlic, finely chopped
1 fennel bulb, outer leaves removed
and finely sliced
1 red chilli, finely chopped (optional)
320g / 11 oz / 1 1/3 cups risotto
(Arborio) rice
100ml / 3 ½ fl oz / ½ cup dry white
wine
1 L / 2 ¼ pints / 4 ¼ cups chicken or
vegetable stock
200g raw prawns (shrimps), shelled
3 tbsp butter
1 lemon, grated zest and juiced
1 tbsp chervil, chopped

- Heat the oil and butter in a large pan and add the onion and garlic. Cook until soft and translucent.
- Add the fennel and stir to coat, then the chilli if using. Add the rice and stir to coat in the butter. Pour in the wine and stir the rice while the wine is absorbed.
- Once the wine has cooked in, reduce the heat a little and add the hot stock, a ladleful at a time, stirring fairly continuously.
- Keep stirring in the stock and tasting the rice. Add the prawns (shrimps) halfway through cooking.
- After about 15-20 minutes the rice should be soft but with a slight bite.
- Season and remove from the heat. Add the butter and leave to melt into the risotto.
- Stir through the lemon zest and juice and chervil and serve immediately.

406

SERVES 4

Carrot and Cashew Risotto

Turnip and Cashew Risotto

407

Use the same amount of turnip as you would carrot.

Carrot and Pine Nut Risotto

408

Change the weight of cashew nuts for pine nuts.

Sweet Carrot Risotto

409

Add 1 tsp of honey to make a sweeter risotto at the end of cooking.

PREPARATION TIME: 15 MINUTES

COOKING TIME: 25 MINUTES

....

INGREDIENTS

2 tbsp olive oil
40 g / 1 oz / ⅓ cup butter
1 onion, peeled and finely chopped
2 cloves garlic, finely chopped
2 celery stalks, finely sliced
2 carrots, peeled and finely diced
320 g / 11 oz / 1 ⅓ cups risotto (Arborio) rice
120 ml / 4 fl. oz / ½ cup dry white wine
1 l / 2 ¼ pints / 4 ¼ cups chicken or vegetable stock
3 tbsp butter
120 g / 4 oz / ½ cup Parmesan, grated
75 g / 2 ½ oz / plain cashew nuts

- Heat the oil and butter in a large pan and add the onion, garlic, celery and carrot. Cook until soft and translucent.
- Add the rice and stir to coat in the butter.
- Pour in the wine and stir the rice while the wine is absorbed.
- Once the wine has cooked in, reduce the heat a little and add the hot stock, a ladleful at a time, stirring fairly continuously. This will give the risotto its creamy texture.
- Keep stirring in the stock and tasting the rice. After about 15-20 minutes, the rice should be soft but with a slight bite. If you run out of stock before the rice is cooked, simply use water.
- Season with salt and pepper and remove from the heat. Add the butter and Parmesan and leave to melt into the risotto.
- Serve immediately with the cashews stirred through.

410

SERVES 4

Risotto with Dublin Bay Prawns

PREPARATION TIME: 5 MINUTES

COOKING TIME: 25 MINUTES

INGREDIENTS

2 tbsp olive oil
40 g / 1 oz / ⅓ cup butter
1 onion, peeled and finely chopped
2 cloves garlic, finely chopped
320 g / 11 oz / 1 ⅓ cups risotto (Arborio) rice
100 ml / 3 ½ fl. oz / ½ cup dry white wine
1 l / 2 ¼ pints / 4 ¼ cups chicken or vegetable stock
250 g / 9 oz / 2 / 3 cup Dublin Bay prawns (shrimps), shell on
120 g / 4 ¼ oz / ¾ cup frozen peas
3 tbsp butter

- Heat the oil and butter in a large pan and add the onion and garlic. Cook until soft and translucent.
- Add the rice and stir to coat in the butter.
- Pour in the wine and stir. Once the wine has cooked, reduce the heat a little and add the hot stock, a ladleful at a time, stirring fairly continuously. This will give the risotto its creamy texture.
- Keep stirring in the stock and tasting the rice.
- 10 minutes before the end of cooking, add the prawns and peas to the pan.
- After about 15-20 minutes the rice should be soft but with a slight bite. If you run out of stock before the rice is cooked, simply use water.
- Season and remove from the heat. Add the butter and leave to melt into the risotto.
- Serve immediately.

Risotto with Mussels

411

Use 400 g / 14 oz / 2 cups mussels, debearded. Add them 5 minutes before the end of cooking and discard any that remain closed.

412

SERVES 4

Spring Risotto with Goat's Cheese

PREPARATION TIME: 15 MINUTES

COOKING TIME: 25 MINUTES

INGREDIENTS

2 tbsp olive oil
40 g / 1 oz / ⅓ cup butter
1 onion, peeled and finely chopped
1 clove garlic, finely chopped
2 celery stalks, finely diced
2 carrots, peeled and finely diced
1 courgette (zucchini), finely diced
100 g broad beans, double podded
75 g / 2 ½ oz / ½ cup peas, frozen or fresh
6 stalks asparagus, woody ends snapped off and cut into short lengths
320 g / 11 oz / 1 ⅓ cups risotto (Arborio) rice
100 ml / 3 ½ fl. oz / ½ cup dry white wine
1 l / 2 ¼ pints / 4 ¼ cups chicken or vegetable stock
3 tbsp butter
120 g / 4 oz / ½ cup goat's cheese

- Heat the oil and butter in a large pan and add the onion, garlic carrot and celery. Cook until soft and translucent.
- Add the courgettes (zucchini) and stir. Add the rice and stir to coat in the butter. Pour in the wine and stir the rice while the wine is absorbed.
- Once the wine has cooked in, reduce the heat a little and add the hot stock, a ladleful at a time, stirring fairly continuously.
- Keep stirring in the stock and tasting the rice. Add the asparagus, peas and beans about 5 minutes before the end of cooking.
- After about 15-20 minutes the rice should be soft but with a slight bite.
- Season and remove from the heat. Add the butter and leave to melt into the risotto.
- Crumble the cheese over the top and serve immediately.

Green Spring Risotto

810

Add ½ pack fine green beans, cut in half added with the courgettes.

413

SERVES 4

Lemon Risotto

- Heat the oil and butter in a large pan and add the onion and celery. Cook until soft and translucent.
- Add the rice and stir to coat in the butter. Pour in the wine and stir the rice while the wine is absorbed.
- Once the wine has cooked in, reduce the heat a little and add the hot stock, a ladleful at a time, stirring fairly continuously.
- Keep stirring in the stock and tasting the rice. After about 15-20 minutes the rice should be soft but with a slight bite.
- Season with salt and pepper and remove from the heat. Add the butter, lemon zest and juice and Parmesan and leave to melt into the risotto.
- Stir through the Mascarpone if using and serve immediately.

PREPARATION TIME: 5 MINUTES

COOKING TIME: 25 MINUTES

INGREDIENTS

2 tbsp olive oil
40 g / 1 oz / ⅓ cup butter
1 onion, peeled and finely chopped
1 celery stalk, peeled and finely sliced
320 g / 11 oz / 1 ⅓ cups risotto (Arborio) rice
100 ml / 3 ½ fl. oz / ½ cup dry white wine
1 l / 2 ¼ pints / 4 ¼ cups chicken or vegetable stock
3 tbsp butter
2 lemons, grated zest and juiced
150 g / 5 oz / 2 / 3 cup Parmesan, grated
3 tbsp Mascarpone, optional

Orange Risotto
414

Use 2 oranges instead of lemons

415

SERVES 4

Red Mullet Risotto

- Heat the oil and butter in a large pan and add the onion and garlic, yellow pepper and celery. Cook until soft.
- Add the rice and stir to coat in the butter. Pour in the wine and stir the rice while the wine is absorbed.
- Once the wine has cooked in, reduce the heat a little and add the hot stock, a ladleful at a time, stirring fairly continuously.
- Keep stirring in the stock and tasting the rice. After about 15-20 minutes the rice should be soft but with a slight bite.
- Meanwhile heat a little oil in a pan and sear the red mullet fillets skin side down until the skin is crisp.
- Remove from the pan and set aside.
- Season the risotto and remove from the heat. Add the butter and leave to melt into the risotto. Lay the fish on top, cover with a lid and leave for a few minutes to cook through. Serve immediately.

PREPARATION TIME: 10 MINUTES

COOKING TIME: 25 MINUTES

INGREDIENTS

8 red mullet fillets, deboned
2 tbsp olive oil
40 g / 1 oz / ⅓ cup butter
1 onion, peeled and finely chopped
2 cloves garlic, finely chopped
2 celery stalks, finely chopped
320 g / 11 oz / 1 ⅓ cups risotto (Arborio) rice
100 ml / 3 ½ fl. oz / ½ cup dry white wine
1 l / 2 ¼ pints / 4 ¼ cups fish stock
3 tbsp butter
1 yellow pepper, deseeded and finely diced

Hake Risotto
416

Use any firm white fish such as hake or sea bream or bass.

417

SERVES 4

Baby Vegetable Risotto with Clams

Vegetable Risotto with Mussels

418

Add 400 g / 14 oz / 2 cups of mussels instead of clams and cook the same.

Baby Vegetable Bass Risotto

419

Fry a fillet of seabass with the asparagus. Put to one side and once the risotto is cooked, flake over the top.

Baby Vegetable Risotto with Prawns

420

Add 100 g / 3 ½ oz / ½ cup of prawns to the Risotto 6 minutes before the end of cooking until pink.

PREPARATION TIME: 15 MINUTES

COOKING TIME: 25 MINUTES

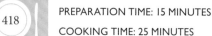

INGREDIENTS

2 tbsp olive oil
40 g / 1 oz / ⅓ cup butter
1 onion, peeled and finely chopped
2 stalks celery, finely chopped
100 g / 3 ½ oz / 2 / 3 cup broad beans, double podded
75 g / 2 ½ oz / ½ cup peas, frozen or fresh
8 stalks asparagus, woody ends snapped off and stalks cut into short lengths
320 g / 11 oz / 1 ⅓ cups risotto (Arborio) rice
100 ml / 3 ½ fl. oz / ½ cup dry white wine
1 l / 2 ¼ pints / 4 ¼ cups chicken or vegetable stock
400 g / 13 ½ oz / 1 ½ cups clams, cleaned
3 tbsp butter
½ lemon, juiced

- Heat the oil and butter in a large pan and add the onion, garlic and celery. Cook until soft and translucent.
- Add the asparagus to the pan and stir to coat.
- Add the rice and stir to coat in the butter.
- Pour in the wine and stir the rice while the wine is absorbed.
- Once the wine has cooked in, reduce the heat a little and add the hot stock, a ladleful at a time, stirring fairly continuously. This will give the risotto its creamy texture.
- Keep stirring in the stock and tasting the rice.
- After about 15-20 minutes the rice should be soft but with a slight bite. If you run out of stock before the rice is cooked, simply use water.
- Halfway through cooking add the peas and beans.
- 5 minutes before the end of cooking add the clams
- Season with black pepper and remove from the heat. Add the butter and leave to melt into the risotto.
- Stir in the lemon juice and serve immediately.

421

SERVES 4

Risotto with Cashews and Mushrooms

- Heat the oil and butter in a large pan and add the onion and garlic. Cook until soft and translucent.
- Add the mushrooms and thyme and cook until the liquid has evaporated. Add the rice and stir to coat in the butter. Pour in the wine and stir the rice while the wine is absorbed.
- Once the wine has cooked in, reduce the heat a little and add the hot stock, a ladleful at a time, stirring fairly continuously.
- Keep stirring in the stock and tasting the rice. After about 15-20 minutes the rice should be soft but with a slight bite.
- Season and remove from the heat. Add the butter and Parmesan and leave to melt into the risotto.
- Stir through the parsley cashew nuts and serve immediately.

Risotto with Hazelnuts

422

Chopped and roasted hazelnuts (cob nuts) would make a nice variation

PREPARATION TIME: 10 MINUTES

COOKING TIME: 25 MINUTES

INGREDIENTS

2 tbsp olive oil
40 g / 1 oz / ⅓ cup butter
1 onion, peeled and finely chopped
2 cloves garlic, finely chopped
200 g / 7 oz / 2 cups mixed wild mushrooms, torn
Small bunch fresh thyme leaves
320 g / 11 oz / 1 ⅓ cups risotto (Arborio) rice
100 ml / 3 ½ fl. oz / ½ cup dry white wine
1 l / 2 ¼ pints / 4 ¼ cups chicken or vegetable stock
3 tbsp butter
120 g / 4 oz / ½ cup Parmesan, grated
2 tbsp parsley, chopped
100 g / 3 ½ oz / 2 / 3 cup cashew nuts, plain

423

SERVES 4

Spicy Chocolate Risotto

- Place the rice in a pan with the milk, cream, 75 g chocolate, cinnamon stick and the whole chilli.
- Bring to a gentle simmer and cook for about 15-20 minutes or until the rice is tender.
- Taste and see if you would like it more chocolatey – add more if necessary.
- Remove the spices and serve with a dollop of Mascarpone.

Spicy White Chocolate Risotto

424

Use the same amount of white chocolate instead.

PREPARATION TIME: 10 MINUTES

COOKING TIME: 15- 20 MINUTES

INGREDIENTS

400 g / 13 ½ oz / 1 ½ cups risotto (Arborio) rice
300 ml / 10 fl. oz / 1 ¼ cups whole milk
300 ml / 10 fl. oz / 1 ¼ cups double (heavy) cream
75 g-100 g dark chocolate, broken into chunks
1 cinnamon stick
1 red chilli, whole
4 tbsp Mascarpone, optional

425

SERVES 6

Veal Casserole with Gremolata

Pork Casserole with Gremolata

426

Substitute cubed pork for the veal

Chilli Veal casserole

427

Add a pinch of dried chilli flakes

Veal with Orange Gremolata

428

Add the zest of 1 orange to the Gremolata for added taste.

PREPARATION TIME: 30 MINUTES

COOKING TIME: 1 HOUR

....

INGREDIENTS

6 tbsp olive oil
1.5kg / 3lbs / 6 cups rose veal, cubed
3 cloves garlic, finely chopped
150 ml / 5 fl. oz / ⅔ cup dry white wine
2 lemons
75 g / 2 ½ oz / ⅓ cup green olives, stoned
1 tbsp parsley, roughly chopped

- Heat 2 tbsp of the oil in a casserole pan and cook the veal until sealed on all sides.
- Add 1 clove garlic, fry for 1 minute and season.
- Cut 1 lemon into quarters and add to the pan with the wine. Stir then cover and cook gently for 45 minutes.
- Meanwhile, zest the remaining lemon, then cut the flesh (not the pith) into small diced pieces.
- Chop the parsley and slice the olives. Place in a bowl with the lemon zest and flesh and the garlic. Add the remianing olive oil, season with blak pepper and mix well.
- Preheat the oven to 180°C / 350F / gas 5.
- Spoon the veal casserole into 6 mini casserole dishes if desired. Sprinkle over the gremolata and cover with a lid. Bake in the oven for 15 minutes.
- Serve hot.

429

SERVES 4

Cod with Pesto Sauce

- Preheat the oven to 180ºC (160º fan) / 350F / gas 5. Place the cod in a roasting tin, drizzled with oil and seasoned.
- Roast for 12 minutes until just flaking.
- Make the sauce: lightly toast the pine nuts in a dry pan until just gold.
- Pound in a pestle and mortar or pulse in a food processor with garlic and basil until you have a paste.
- Stir in the Parmesan and loosen with oil. Adjust the seasoning.
- Serve the cod on top of the pesto sauce with boiled new potatoes.

PREPARATION TIME 10 MINUTES

COOKING TIME 12 MINUTES

....

INGREDIENTS

4 cod steaks
olive oil
salt and pepper
For the pesto sauce:
small handful pine nuts
1 clove of garlic, peeled and chopped
3 big handfuls basil leaves, chopped
2 tbsp Parmesan, grated
olive oil

430

SERVES 4

Sicilian-style Red Tuna

- Peel the tomatoes by plunging them into boiling water for 20 seconds, then removing the skins. Set aside.
- Add 2 tbsp olive oil to a large pan. Add the onions and pepper and cook until softened and slightly coloured.
- Add the garlic, rosemary and chilli and fry for 2 minutes. Add the capers, anchovies and spices and cook until the anchovies start to melt in the pan.
- Add the chickpeas, chopped and fresh tomatoes and bring to a simmer. When bubbling, add the tuna fillet and push down into the sauce so it is covered.
- Cover partially with a lid and leave to simmer gently for about 20-25 minutes. You want it very nearly cooked through but still blushing pink.
- When cooked, remove the tuna from the pan and adjust the seasoning.
- To serve, slice the tuna and lay on a platter, then spoon over the sauce. Serve with bread.

PREPARATION TIME: 20 MINUTES

COOKING TIME: 45 MINUTES

....

INGREDIENTS

1 kg / 2 lbs / 4 ½ cups tomatoes
400 g / 13 ½ oz fresh tuna fillet
2 tbsp olive oil
1 red onion, peeled and thickly sliced
1 green pepper, 'cheeks' cut off
1 red pepper, 'cheeks' cut off
4 cloves garlic, finely sliced
2 sprigs rosemary leaves
1 chilli, finely chopped
2 tbsp capers, drained
5 anchovy fillets
1 tsp dried oregano
1 cinnamon stick
1 tsp ground cumin
400 g / 14 oz / 2 cups chickpeas (garbanzo beans), drained
400 g / 14 oz / 2 cups chopped tomatoes

Citrus Red Tuna

431

A slice of orange peel (no pith) gives a slightly citrusy twist to the sauce. Add with the tomatoes.

432

SERVES 4

Calabrian Stuffed Squid

Chilli Stuffed Squid 433

Add a little finely chopped red chilli to the sauce

Squid with Caper Sauce 434

Add 2 tsp capers to the sauce

Tuna Stuffed Squid 435

Replace the 3 anchovy fillets with 1 can of tuna.

PREPARATION TIME: 15 MINUTES

COOKING TIME: 30 MINUTES

....

INGREDIENTS

4 squid, cleaned and ink sac removed

FOR THE FILLING

1 tbsp olive oil
3 anchovy fillets
2 cloves garlic, chopped
2 celery stalks, finely diced
1 aubergine (eggplant), finely diced
400 g / 14 oz / 2 cups chopped tomatoes
1 tbsp basil, finely chopped
½ orange, grated zest
1 tbsp live oil

- Pat the squid dry and set aside.
- Heat the oil in a pan and melt the anchovy fillets with the garlic.
- Add the celery and aubergine (eggplant) and cook for 10 minutes, or until softened.
- Add the whole tomatoes
- Stir in the basil and zest, season and cook for 10 minutes until reduced.
- Spoon the tomato sauce into the squid and secure with a toothpick.
- Sear in a hot pan with the remaining oil then cook gently for about 5-10 minutes until just cooked through.
- Serve hot.

436

SERVES 4

Italian-style Chicken Kiev

- Using a sharp knife, cut a pocket in the side of each chicken breast.
- Use a teaspoon to stuff the pocket with pesto, then press the edges firmly together.
- Place the flour, eggs and polenta on separate plates. Season the flour with salt and pepper.
- Dip each chicken breast into the flour, then the eggs, then the polenta, coating thoroughly each time.
- Heat the butter until foaming then add the chicken breasts and cook, turning regularly for about 20 minutes until cooked through.
- Serve hot with a salad.

PREPARATION TIME: 10 MINUTES

COOKING TIME: 20 MINUTES

INGREDIENTS

4 chicken breasts, skinned
8 tbsp pesto
75 g / 2 ¾ oz / ⅓ cup plain (all purpose) flour
3 eggs, beaten
250 g / 9 oz / 1 cup polenta
2 tbsp butter

Mozzarella Chicken Kiev

437

Add 1 slice of mozzarella with the pesto inside the chicken breast.

438

SERVES 4

Veal Osso Buco with Tomatoes

- Heat the olive oil in a casserole pan and cook the onions and carrots until soft.
- Add the garlic and cook for a minute, then the tomatoes, sage leaves, bouquet garni, chopped basil and the citrus zest. Reduce the heat and cook over a very gentle heat for 15 minutes or so.
- Dredge the veal slices in flour and sear in a hot pan for 2 minutes on each side in a little oil.
- Add to the casserole pan.
- Deglaze the frying pan with the white wine, scraping the base with a wooden spoon then pour into the casserole.
- Crumble in the stock cube, top up with water, cover with a lid and cook gently for 1 hour 30 minutes.
- Remove the veal from the casserole, adjust the seasoning and serve with cooked tagliatelle.

PREPARATION TIME: 20 MINUTES

COOKING TIME:
1 HOUR 50 MINUTES

INGREDIENTS

1.2 kg / 2 lb rose veal shin, cut into thick slices
3 tbsp olive oil
2 onions, peeled and finely chopped
200 g / 6 ½ oz / ¾ cup carrots, finely chopped
1 orange, grated zest
1 lemon, grated zest
1 clove garlic, finely chopped
400 g / 14 oz / 2 cups chopped tomatoes
4 sage leaves, chopped
1 bouquet garni
1 small bunch basil
2 tbsp plain (all purpose) flour
200 ml / 6 ½ fl. oz / ¾ cup dry white wine
1 chicken stock cube

Veal with Balsamic Tomatoes

439

Add 1 tbsp balsamic vinegar at the end of cooking.

440

SERVES 4

Piccata Veal with Duck Foie Gras

PREPARATION TIME: 15 MINUTES

COOKING TIME: 10-15 MINUTES

....

INGREDIENTS

4 rose veal escalopes
4 slices Parma ham
1 ball mozzarella
150 g / 5 oz / 2 / 3 cup duck liver pate
4 sage leaves
4 tbsp plain (all purpose) flour
2 eggs, beaten
4 tbsp polenta
2 tbsp olive oil

- Place the veal escalopes between 2 pieces clingfilm (plastic wrap) and bat out gently with a rolling pin until quite thin.
- Lay a slice of ham, 2 slices mozzarella and a slice of pate on one half of each escalope, then press a sage leaf on top.
- Fold over the other half of the escalope and secure with a toothpick.
- Dredge with the flour, then the eggs and coat in polenta.
- Heat the oil in a pan and cook gently on both sides until golden brown – approximately 10-15 minutes.

Piccata Pork with Foie Gras

441

Replace the veal with pork fillet, season and cook for the same length of time.

442

SERVES 4

Liver with Polenta

PREPARATION TIME: 10 MINUTES

COOKING TIME: 55 MINUTES

....

INGREDIENTS

225 g / 9 oz / 1 cup polenta
1.7 l / 3 pints / 6 cups water
100 g / 3 ½ oz / ½ cup butter
6 tbsp Parmesan, grated
2 tbsp butter
3 onions, peeled and sliced
1 tbsp sugar
275 ml / 10 fl. oz / I cup Marsala
1 tbsp butter
250 g / 9 oz calves' liver, thickly sliced

- Whisk the polenta into a pan of boiling salted water. As soon as it begins to boil, turn the heat down to and stir every 5 minutes.
- Cook for 45 minutes until it has the consistency of mashed potato. Season with salt and pepper. Stir in the butter and Parmesan and adjust the seasoning. Keep warm and set aside.
- Meanwhile, heat the butter in a pan and when foaming add the onions. Reduce the heat and cook very slowly until deep gold and sweet. Add the sugar after about 10 minutes to help the caramelisation.
- Pour in the Marsala and reduce until syrupy. Season and set aside.
- Heat the remaining butter in a pan and fry the calves' liver for 1-2 minutes until still pink in the centre.
- Serve on the polenta with the sauce spooned over.

Venetian Liver with Capers

443

Add 2 tsp capers for piquancy

Balsamic Liver with Polenta

444

Add ½ tbsp balsamic vinegar for added depth of flavour with the Marsala.

445

SERVES 4

Chicken Arrabiata

Chicken Arrabiata with Olives

446

Add a handful chopped black olives to the sauce.

Turkey Arrabiata

447

Swap the chicken for turkey and cook this dish the same.

Chicken Arrabiata with Sun-dried Tomatoes

448

On the top of this dish add 2 large sundried tomatoes for flavour.

PREPARATION TIME: 10 MINUTES

COOKING TIME: 15 MINUTES

INGREDIENTS

300 g penne pasta
2 tbsp olive oil
2 chicken breasts, skinned and cubed
2 cloves garlic, chopped
1 red chilli, finely chopped
400 g / 14 oz / 2 cups chopped tomatoes
2 tbsp basil, chopped

- Cook the pasta in boiling salted water according to packet instructions, then drain, toss with a little oil and set aside.
- Meanwhile heat the olive oil in a pan and fry the chicken briskly until golden on all sides.
- Add the garlic and chilli and fry for 1 minute, then tip in the tomatoes.
- Add a splash of water and cook for 10 minutes, or until the chicken is cooked and the sauce is reduced.
- Stir through the basil, then stir in the pasta.
- Serve hot.

449

SERVES 4

Monkfish and Lemon Osso Buco

PREPARATION TIME: 10 MINUTES

COOKING TIME: 35 MINUTES

INGREDIENTS

2 tbsp olive oil
1 onion, peeled and finely chopped
2 cloves garlic, finely chopped
4 plum tomatoes, chopped
1 tbsp tomato puree
4 monkfish steaks
200 ml / 6 ½ fl. oz / ¾ cup dry white wine
8 asparagus stalks, woody ends snapped off
½ lemon, grated zest
1 tbsp parsley, chopped

- Heat the olive oil in a casserole pan and gently fry the onion and garlic until translucent.
- Add the tomatoes and puree and cook for a few minutes until the tomatoes have collapsed.
- Add the monkfish and colour on both sides before pouring over the white wine. Season with salt and pepper and reduce the heat right down. Cover with a lid and simmer for 15 minutes very gently.
- Cut the asparagus into short lengths and add to the pan with the lemon zest and cook until just tender – 8 minutes or so.
- Remove the monkfish when cooked and stir in the parsley. Reduce the sauce if it's a little thin.
- Serve the fish with tagliatelle spoon over the sauce

450

SERVES 4

Rabbit with Olives and Capers

PREPARATION TIME: 10 MINUTES

COOKING TIME:
1 HOUR 45 MINUTES

INGREDIENTS

1 rabbit, jointed
2 tbsp oil
1 onion, peeled and chopped
2 celery stalks, chopped
1 carrot, peeled and chopped
2 cloves garlic, chopped
1 lemon, grated zest and juiced
200 ml / 6 ½ fl. oz / ¾ cup dry white wine
2 tbsp capers, drained
Handful green olives, chopped
225 g / 9 oz / 1 cup polenta
1.7 l / 3 pints / 6 cups water

- Preheat the oven to 150°C / 300F / gas 2.
- Heat the oil in a casserole pan and cook the vegetables until soft and the onion translucent.
- Add the rabbit, turn the heat up and cook until sealed on all sides.
- Add the lemon zest and a little juice and the wine and add a little water to nearly cover the rabbit. Add the capers and olives and stir.
- Cover with a lid and cook in the oven for at least 1 hour 30 minutes until the rabbit is completely tender. Remove from the oven and set aside when cooked.
- Meanwhile, whisk the polenta slowly into a large pan of boiling salted water.
- As soon as it begins to boil, stir every 5 minutes, ensuring you push the spoon down into the sides of the pan.
- Cook for about 45 minutes until it begins to have the consistency of mashed potato. Season with salt and pepper.
- Oil a tray and tip the polenta out onto to it. Spread the polenta to about 2.5cm / 1" thick. Leave the polenta to cool for about 30 minutes. Cut into circles and griddle for a minute either side to reheat and colour.
- Serve with the rabbit pieces and the sauce.

451

SERVES 4

Chicken Pilaff with Mussels

PREPARATION TIME: 10 MINUTES

COOKING TIME: 35 MINUTES

....

INGREDIENTS

2 tbsp olive oil
1 onion, peeled and finely chopped
2 cloves garlic, finely chopped
4 chicken thighs, skinned
½ red chilli, chopped
250 g / 9 oz / 1 cup basmati rice
550 ml / 1 pint / 2 cups chicken stock
400 g / 14 oz / 2 cups chopped
tomatoes
Pinch saffron
250 g / 9 oz / 1 cup mussels, cleaned
½ lemon, juiced

- Heat the oil in a casserole and sweat the onion and garlic until soft.
- Add the chicken thighs and chilli and seal chicken on both sides.
- Add the rice, then pour in the stock and tomatoes and stir well. Crumble in the saffron, season with salt and pepper and cover with a lid.
- Simmer gently for approximately 20 minutes until the liquid has been mostly absorbed – if it looks a little dry add more water.
- Add the mussels, put the lid back on and cook until the mussels have all opened. Discard any that remain closed.
- Squeeze over the lemon and serve with cooked green beans.

Chicken Pilaff with Prawns

452

Substitute the mussels for shell-on prawns (shrimps)

453

SERVES 4

Confit Lamb Caramellone

PREPARATION TIME 2 HOURS

COOKING TIME 2 HOURS
5 MINUTES

INGREDIENTS

1 lamb shoulder, on the bone
2 cloves of garlic, peeled
1 sprig rosemary
salt and pepper
For the pasta verde:
250 g / ½ lb / 1 cup "00" flour
2 eggs
250 g / ½ lb / 1 cup spinach wilted,
squeezed and cooled, finely chopped
For the pasta rossa:
250 g / ½ lb / 1 cup '00' flour
3 eggs
2 tbsp tomato paste
100 g sultanas or raisins soaked in a
little Marsala
tomato sauce, to serve

- Bring a pan of water to the boil. Add garlic, rosemary and lamb and bring to the boil.
- Reduce the heat and simmer for 2 hours. Remove the lamb and leave to cool.
- Place flour in a bowl and make a well, then crack the eggs into the well.
- Mix the eggs and spinach, and then add flour.
- Remove the dough and knead for 5 minutes. Repeat for the pasta rossa.
- Cover with clingfilm and rest for 30 minutes in the refrigerator.
- When the lamb is cool, shred the meat. Remove the pasta from the fridge and roll the dough into sheets 2mm thick and 10cm wide.
- Lay on a floured surface. Cut out squares of pasta 4 x 5cm. Place 1 tbsp of lamb with sultanas in each square, then roll the pasta up.
- Seal the edges, then squeeze and twist the ends. Place on parchment, cover with a tea towel and repeat.
- Cook in boiling salted water for 5 minutes then remove and serve with tomato sauce.

454

SERVES 4

Veal Stew with Rigatoni

- Cook the broad beans in boiling water for 2 minutes then drain. Leave to cool then remove the skins. Set aside.
- Heat 2 tbsp oil in a pan and brown the cubed veal in batches with the garlic.
- Add the onions and leave to cook slowly until golden then add the white wine. Cook gently for 15 minutes.
- Add the beans and 2 tbsp chopped chervil and cook for another 5 minutes.
- Stir in the creme fraiche and season. Stir through the lemon zest at the last minute.
- Cook the pasta in boiling salted water according to packet instructions. Drain and serve with the veal.

PREPARATION TIME 25 MINUTES

COOKING TIME 30 MINUTES

....

INGREDIENTS

300 g / 10 oz / 1 ¼ cups broad beans, podded
olive oil
1 clove garlic, finely chopped
800 g / 1 ¼ lb / 3 cups veal shoulder or shin, cubed
2 onions, finely chopped
1 glass dry white wine
200 ml / 6 ½ fl oz / ¾ cup creme fraiche
300 g / 10 oz / 1 ¼ cups rigatoni pasta
1 bunch chervil
salt and pepper
zest of ½ lemon

455

SERVES 4

Italian Chicken

- Marinate the chicken with a little oil and lemon juice for no longer than 30 minutes.
- Meanwhile heat the oil in a pan and cook the onion and garlic until golden.
- Add the peppers and courgette and cook until golden in patches.
- Add the tomatoes, sugar and seasoning and allow simmering for about 15-20 minutes.
- Meanwhile heat a griddle pan and cook the chicken skin side down until the skin is crisp and golden.
- Turn and cook on the other side for about 5 minutes until the chicken is cooked through.
- Serve with the tomato sauce and chopped basil scattered over.
- Tear a ball of mozzarella into chunks and stir through the sauce just before serving.

PREPARATION TIME 30 MINUTES

COOKING TIME 30 MINUTES

....

INGREDIENTS

4 chicken breasts
olive oil
lemon juice
For the sauce:
2 tbsp olive oil
1 onion, chopped
1 clove of garlic, chopped
1 red pepper, 'cheeks' cut off and chopped
1 yellow pepper, 'cheeks' cut off and chopped
1 courgette, thickly sliced
2 x 400 g can tomatoes
1 tsp sugar
salt and pepper
1 bunch basil

456

SERVES 4

Veal Marengo

PREPARATION TIME 20 MINUTES

COOKING TIME I HOUR
20 MINUTES

INGREDIENTS

1kg / 2 ¼ lb / 4 ¼ cups veal shoulder, deboned
2 carrots, peeled and diced
2 onions, peeled and chopped
2 cloves of garlic, crushed
200 g / 6 ½ oz / ¾ cup button mushrooms, finely chopped
400 g / 13 ½ oz tomatoes, skinned and deseeded and chopped
2 tbsp olive oil
2 tbsp butter
1 bouquet garni
1 tbsp tomato puree
150ml / 5 fl oz / ⅔ cup white wine
salt and pepper

- Cut the veal into cubes.
- Heat the oil in a large casserole with the butter. Brown the veal cubes in batches, then add the carrots, garlic, onion and bouquet garni.
- Cook for 10 minutes, stirring regularly, then add the tomato concasse, puree and mushrooms.
- Cook for 5 minutes then stir in the white wine.
- Season, cover and cook very gently for about 50 minutes.
- Check the veal is tender, then serve with fresh pasta noodles.

457

SERVES 4

Italian-Style Squid

PREPARATION TIME: 10 MINUTES

COOKING TIME: 45 MINUTES

INGREDIENTS

2 tbsp olive oil
2 celery stalks, chopped
2 cloves garlic, chopped
6 ripe tomatoes, chopped
1 squid, cleaned and ink sac removed
200 ml / 6 ½ fl. oz / ¾ cup white wine
½ lemon, juiced

- Heat the olive oil in a pan and fry the celery until soft.
- Add the garlic and tomatoes and cook until the tomatoes collapse a little.
- Cut the squid into pieces and pat dry. Add to the pan with the white wine and a little seasoning.
- Stir well, then partially cover and leave to simmer gently for around 30-45 minutes or until the squid is tender. Top up with water if the pan looks dry.
- Season with lemon juice and serve with a salad or bread.

Italian-style Squid with Chilli
458
Add 1 red chilli, chopped for heat

Italian-style Squid with Prawns
459
Add a handful raw prawns (shrimps) 5 minutes before the end of cooking.

460

SERVES 6

Lamb and Olive Stew

- Heat the oil in a casserole pan and seal the lamb cubes in batches until deep brown.
- Remove from the pan to a bowl and set aside.
- Add the onions and cook until soft, then add the white wine.
- Return the meat to the pan, add the potatoes, tomatoes, olives, paprika and the rosemary leaves.
- Season with salt and pepper, stir well and cover. Cook very gently for 1 hour 45 minutes.

Lamb with Orange Zest

 461

Add a strip of orange zest with the potatoes.

Lamb with Polenta

462

Serve with grilled polenta instead of including potatoes in the stew

PREPARATION TIME: 30 MINUTES

COOKING TIME: 2 HOURS

INGREDIENTS

6 tbsp olive oil
1.2kg / 2 lbs / 5 cups lamb shoulder, deboned
2 onions, peeled and finely chopped
200 ml / 6 ½ fl. oz / ¾ cup white wine
150 g / 5 oz / 2 / 3 cup mixed black and green olives
12 new potatoes
4 tomatoes, diced
½ tsp paprika
1 sprig rosemary

463

SERVES 2

Veal Risotto

- Combine the onion, celery, carrot and rosemary leaves in a food processor until very finely chopped.
- Heat the oil in a pan and fry the mixture gently until soft.
- Turn up the heat, add the veal and fry briskly until golden.
- Add the rice, stir well then pour in the wine and stir until absorbed.
- Continue with the stock, adding a little at a time, stirring well and allowing it to absorb before adding the next ladle.
- Once the rice is tender, season and add the cinnamon.
- Serve hot.

Veal and Courgette Risotto

 464

Add 1 courgette (zucchini), finely diced with the vegetable mix

PREPARATION TIME: 5 MINUTES

COOKING TIME: 40 MINUTES

INGREDIENTS

2 tbsp olive oil
1 onion, peeled and chopped
1 celery stalk, chopped
1 carrot, peeled and chopped
1 sprig rosemary leaves
250 g / 6 ½ oz / ¾ cup minced rose veal
160 g / 5 ½ oz / 2 / 3 cup risotto (Arborio) rice
120 ml / 4 fl. oz / ½ cup dry white wine
500 ml / 1 pint / 2 cups chicken stock
1 tsp ground cinnamon

465

SERVES 4

Cod with Tomato Sauce and Potatoes

Haddock with Tomato Sauce

466

Try this with any firm white fish such as hake or haddock

Cod with Rosemary in Tomato Sauce

467

Sprinkle the potatoes with chopped rosemary halfway through cooking.

Hake in Tomato Sauce

468

Replace the Cod with the same amount of Hake fish.

PREPARATION TIME: 10 MINUTES

COOKING TIME: 25-30 MINUTES

INGREDIENTS

4 tbsp olive oil
4 large baking / floury potatoes, peeled and cut into thin rounds
1 clove garlic, unpeeled and lightly crushed
4 cod steaks
2 tbsp plain (all purpose) flour

FOR THE SAUCE

1 onion, peeled and chopped
½ carrot, peeled and chopped
1 celery stalk, chopped
1 clove garlic, peeled
2 tbsp olive oil
400 g / 14 oz / 2 cups chopped tomatoes
Small handful basil leaves
Pinch dried chilli flakes
½ lemon, grated zest

- Make the sauce first by combining the onion, carrot, celery and garlic in a food processor until very finely chopped.
- Heat the oil in a pan and sweat the vegetables until soft.
- Add the tomatoes and basil and leave to simmer for approximately 15 minutes until reduced.
- Season and stir through the chilli flakes and lemon zest.
- Meanwhile, heat the oil in a large pan and add the potatoes and garlic.
- Season with salt and pepper and leave to cook until crisp on one side (approximately 10 minutes) then turn with a spatula and leave to crisp on the other side.
- Once the potatoes are golden and crisp, remove onto kitchen paper to drain, then keep warm.
- Dredge the cod in the flour then fry in the same pan for around 3-4 minutes per side, depending on the thickness of the fish.
- Once the cod is just cooked through and opaque, serve with the potatoes and sauce spooned over the top.

Rabbit with Lemon and Olives

SERVES 4 · 469

- Marinade the rabbit in buttermilk for at least 1 hour. This helps make the meat tender and juicy.
- Pat dry. Dip into the flour, then egg, then flour again.
- Heat the oil in a large pan and add the rabbit in batches with the lemon pieces.
- Cook the rabbit until golden and just cooked all the way through, removing each batch to kitchen paper before adding the next.
- Once all is cooked, throw the olives into the pan with the sage and sizzle quickly before tipping over the rabbit.

PREPARATION TIME: I HOUR

COOKING TIME: 30 MINUTES

INGREDIENTS

1 rabbit, jointed
250 ml / 9 fl. oz / 1 cup buttermilk
4 tbsp flour, seasoned with salt and a pinch Cayenne pepper
2 eggs, beaten
4 tbsp olive oil
1 lemon, cut into pieces
2 handfuls black olives
4 sage leaves

Chicken with Lemon and Olives · 470

Use chicken joints instead of rabbit, but they will take longer to cook.

Rabbit in White Wine and Olives · 471

Use 120 ml / 4 fl. oz / ½ cup of dry white wine to deglaze the pan for a sauce to accompany.

Chicken Mozzarella Parcels

SERVES 4 · 472

- Place the chicken between 2 pieces of clingfilm (plastic wrap) and bat out until a bit thinner with a rolling pin.
- Using a sharp knife, cut a pocket into the side of each chicken.
- Stuff the pocket with mozzarella and close the edges of the chicken back over to enclose the cheese.
- Season with salt and pepper, then dunk each piece into flour, then egg then the breadcrumbs.
- Heat the oil in a large pan and fry until the chicken is golden and crisp and cooked through – approximately 8-10 minutes.
- Serve with tomatoes.

PREPARATION TIME: 20 MINUTES

COOKING TIME: 10 MINUTES

INGREDIENTS

4 chicken breasts, skinned
1 ball mozzarella, sliced
3 tbsp plain (all purpose) flour
2 eggs, beaten
200 g / 6 ½ oz / ¾ cup breadcrumbs
2 tbsp olive oil
100 g / 3 ½ oz / ½ cup cherry tomatoes, to serve

Chicken Mozzarella and Pesto Parcels · 473

Smear pesto on the mozzarella before stuffing the chicken

474

SERVES 4

Rabbit with Tomatoes and Cous Cous

PREPARATION TIME: 5 MINUTES

COOKING TIME: 25 MINUTES

INGREDIENTS

1 rabbit, jointed
450 g / 16 oz / 2 cups cherry tomatoes
2 sprigs rosemary
2 tbsp olive oil
250 g / 9 oz / 1 cup cous cous
250 ml / 9 fl. oz / 1 cup chicken stock
½ lemon, juiced

- Preheat the oven to 180°C / 350F / gas 6.
- Place the rabbit in a roasting tin with tomatoes snugly around, add the rosemary, season and toss with oil.
- Roast for about 25 minutes until cooked through. Set aside to rest.
- Meanwhile, place the cous cous in a bowl, cover with the hot stock and clingfilm (plastic wrap) the bowl. Leave for 10 minutes or so until tender, then fork through the grains and add the lemon juice.
- Serve with the rabbit, tomatoes and roasting juices spooned over.

Rabbit with Tomatoes and Olives

475

Add handful black olives to the roasting tin while resting

Rabbit with Tomatoes and Sultanas

476

Add a handful sultanas to the cous cous while soaking

477

SERVES 4

Escalope Milanese with Tagliatelle

PREPARATION TIME: 10 MINUTES

COOKING TIME: 10 MINUTES

INGREDIENTS

4 rose veal escalopes
2 tbsp plain (all purpose) flour
2 eggs, beaten
6 tbsp breadcrumbs
3 tbsp olive oil or butter
1 lemon, sliced
300 g / 10 oz / 1 ¼ cups fresh tagliatelle
1 tbsp butter
2 tbsp flat leaf parsley, chopped

- Place the escalopes between 2 pieces clingfilm (plastic wrap) and bat out until thin with a rolling pin.
- Dredge each escalope in the flour, egg and then breadcrumbs.
- Heat the oil or butter in a pan and when smoking, add the veal.
- Cook on both sides until golden brown – approximately 3 minutes per side.
- Meanwhile cook the tagliatelle in boiling salted water according to packet instructions. Drain and toss with a little butter and chopped parsley.
- Serve with slices of lemon.

Escalope Milanese with Tomatoes

478

Toss the tagliatelle with 2 chopped tomatoes

479

SERVES 6

Rabbit with Chorizo

- Remove the outer skin from the spring onions. Finely chop 2 of them.
- Heat half the butter with the oil in a pan and add the chopped onion and rabbit and seal the rabbit on both sides. Add the remaining whole onions, chorizo, season with salt and pepper and cook on low for 45 minutes.
- Bring 1 ¼ l water to the boil with salt. Stir in the polenta and cook for 5 minutes stirring continuously, then add a little black pepper and remove from the heat when the polenta starts to come away from the sides of the pan.
- Mix in 20 g butter and then turn onto a greased platter and smooth out until 1cm thick. Leave to cool then cut into squares.
- Heat the remaining butter in a pan and colour the polenta on both sides.
- Drain on kitchen paper then serve with the rabbit, chorizo and onions.

PREPARATION TIME: 20 MINUTES

COOKING TIME: 1 HOUR

INGREDIENTS

6 spring onions (scallions)
70 g / 2 ½ oz / ¼ cup butter
6 saddles of rabbit
150 g / 5 oz / 2 / 3 cup chorizo, chopped
250 g / 9 oz / 1 cup polenta
2 tbsp olive oil
200 ml / 6 ½ fl. oz / ¾ cup white wine

480

SERVES 4

Fregola cun Cocciula

- Cook the pasta according to packet instructions.
- Heat the oil in a pan and cook the garlic, parsley and chilli for 1 minute.
- Add the clams and fish stock and cook for 3-5 minutes until all the clams have opened. Discard any that remain closed.
- Carefully pour the clams and most of the liquor into another pan, being careful to leave any sand or sediment at the bottom of the pan.
- Toss with the pasta and serve.

PREPARATION TIME: 5 MINUTES

COOKING TIME: 10 MINUTES

INGREDIENTS

4 tbsp olve oil
2 cloves garlic, chopped
4 tbsp parsley, chopped
1 tsp chilli flakes
250 ml / 9 fl. oz / 1 cup fish stock
250 g / 9 oz / 1 cup fregola pasta
1 kg / 2 lb / 4 ¼ cups clams

481

SERVES 4

Mozzarella and Parma Ham Panini

PREPARATION TIME: 20 MINUTES

COOKING TIME: 10 MINUTES

INGREDIENTS

6 ripe tomatoes, thickly sliced
1 tsp thyme leaves
4 panini rolls
2 tbsp olive oil
1 clove garlic, cut in half
2 balls mozzarella, drained
8 slices prosciutto or San Daniele ham

- Lay the tomatoes in a dish and season. Drizzle with oil and thyme leaves and leave to macerate for 10 minutes.
- If the Panini rolls require cooking, do so according to packet instructions.
- Once cool, slice in half and brush with oil from the tomatoes and the cut garlic clove. Lightly toast the cut sides until golden.
- Layer the tomatoes, ham and mozzarella in the Panini rolls then serve.

Wrapped Mozzarella Panini

482

Wrap the filled rolls in foil and bake until the mozzarella oozes

Prosciutto and Taleggio Panini

483

Use Taleggio for a stronger flavour

484

SERVES 4

Sicilian Swordfish with Pasta

PREPARATION TIME: 5 MINUTES

COOKING TIME: 10 MINUTES

INGREDIENTS

4 swordfish steaks, of equal thickness
3 tbsp olive oil
1 orange, grated zest and juice
2 tbsp sultanas
2 tbsp pine nuts, lightly toasted
120 ml / 4 fl. oz / ½ cup dry white wine
300 g / 10 ½ oz / 1 ½ cups cooked pasta, to serve

- Cook the pasta according to packet instructions. Drain toss with 1 tbsp olive oil and set aside.
- Heat 2 tbsp of oil in a pan and sear the swordfish on both sides until lightly coloured.
- Add the zest and juice of the orange, sultanas and wine and season with salt and pepper. Cook at a simmer until the swordfish is cooked through – approximately 5 minutes.
- Remove the fish from the pan and reduce the cooking juices, adding the pine nuts at the last minute.
- Serve the fish with the cooked pasta and the sauce spooned over.

Sicilian Tuna with Pasta

485

Use tuna steaks instead of swordfish

Sicilian Swordfish with Capers

486

Add 1 tsp capers to the finished sauce.

487

SERVES 4

Succulent Rose Veal

- Preheat oven to 100°C / 200F. Heat the oil in a casserole pan and sear the veal on both sides. Add the onion to the pan then pour in the stock and add the herbs.
- Cover with a lid and cook in the oven for about 4 hours until the meat is completely tender. Once cooked, season the veal medallions with salt and pepper.
- Heat the butter and oil in a pan and cook the medallions for 3 minutes on each side, adding the garlic and thyme halfway through cooking. Spoon the butter over the steaks as they cook.
- Remove to a plate to rest and deglaze the pan with sherry. Reduce to a syrupy consistency and set aside.
- Cook the mushrooms in the butter and garlic until tender, then wilt the spinach into the mushrooms and add the artichokes.
- Place a square of veal cheek and a veal medallion on a plate and pour over the sauce. Serve with the vegetables.

Breadcrumb Covered Veal
488

Once cooked through, try bread-crumbing one side of the veal cheek and pan-frying until crisp and golden.

PREPARATION TIME: 20 MINUTES

COOKING TIME:
4 HOURS 15 MINUTES

....

INGREDIENTS

1 kg / 2 lbs rose veal cheeks or breast, cut into 4 equal pieces
2 tbsp olive oil
1 onion, halved
1 l / 2 pints / 6 cups chicken stock
1 sprig rosemary
1 sprig thyme
4 175 g / 6 oz rose veal fillets
1 tbsp butter, 2 tbsp olive oil
5 cloves garlic, lightly crushed
1 tbsp thyme leaves
100 ml / 3 ½ fl. oz / ½ cup dry sherry
2 tbsp butter
1 handful wild mushrooms
1 clove garlic, chopped
250 g / 9 oz / 1 cup spinach leaves
1 handful artichoke hearts

489

SERVES 4

Cod with Stuffed Potatoes

- Preheat the oven to 180ºC (160º fan) / 350F / gas 5. Boil the potatoes in salted water until completely tender. Drain and leave to cool a little.
- Meanwhile place the cod in a roasting tin, drizzle with oil, season and cook for about 12 minutes.
- Mix the herbs, anchovies and garlic in a food processor, drizzling in a little oil to make a paste.
- Halve the potatoes and scoop out a little to make a well in the centre.
- Fill the well with 1 tsp of herby filling. Place the tops back on and place in the oven just to heat through.
- Serve with the cod and drizzled with olive oil.

PREPARATION TIME 20 MINUTES

COOKING TIME 12 MINUTES

....

INGREDIENTS

4 cod steaks
olive oil
salt and pepper
16 medium-sized potatoes
½ bunch parsley
½ bunch basil
4 anchovies
1 clove of garlic, peeled

500 RECIPES • ITALIAN

Stuffed Pheasant

490
SERVES 4

Stuffed Chicken 491

Use chicken instead of pheasant.

Stuffed Turkey 492

Instead of using pheasant, replace with 1 turkey, cleaned and untrussed.

Stuffed Pheasant with 493
Parma Ham Fingers

Substitute the Polenta fingers for Parma ham instead.

PREPARATION TIME: 25 MINUTES

COOKING TIME: 1 HOUR

INGREDIENTS

FOR THE STUFFING
2 tbsp butter
500 g / 1lb / 2 cups wild mushrooms
1 onion, finely chopped
1 clove garlic, chopped
1 tbsp pine nuts
10 chestnuts, chopped
1 tbsp parsley, chopped
1 slice bread, soaked in milk
1 egg, beaten
1 pheasant, cleaned and untrussed
2 tbsp butter, softened

• Heat the butter in a pan and cook the mushrooms and onions until soft.
• Add the garlic, pine nuts and chestnuts and stir well.
• Transfer to a bowl and mix in the parsley, crumble in the bread then mix in the egg. Use your hands to combine everything.
• Stuff the pheasant with the mixture, then secure the openings with toothpicks to prevent it falling out. Any extra stuffing can be baked in a roasting tin alongside.
• Preheat the oven to 200°C / 400F / gas 6. Place the pheasant in a tin and rub all over with softened butter and season with salt and pepper.
• Roast in the oven for about an hour, covering with foil if it looks like burning.
• Leave to rest for 10 minutes before carving. Serve with polenta fingers.

140

494

SERVES 4-6

Rabbit Terrine with Prune Jelly

- Preheat the oven to 150°C / 300F / gas 1. Pulse the meat in a food processor until a coarse mince is formed.
- Turn into a bowl and mix thoroughly with the remaining terrine ingredients. Spoon into a lined loaf tin or baking dish and wrap securely in foil.
- Place in a roasting tin and fill half way up the sides of the tin with boiling water. Bake in the oven for 90 minutes, then leave to cool.
- Place weights on top of the terrine and compress in the refrigerator for 24 hours.
- The next day make the jelly. Soak the gelatine in cold water until softened – squeeze out.
- Heat the prune juice, and stir in the gelatine, whisking until dissolved.
- Pour the jelly onto the terrine. Push the tarragon, garlic and olives into the jelly.
- Refrigerate until set, then serve in slices.

PREPARATION TIME: I DAY

COOKING TIME: 90 MINUTES

....

INGREDIENTS

FOR THE TERRINE
Meat from 1 rabbit
200 g / 6 ½ oz / ¾ cup chicken livers
200 g / 6 ½ oz / ¾ cup pork belly
1 tbsp thyme leaves
2 cloves garlic, crushed
½ lemon, grated zest

FOR THE PRUNE JELLY
3 leaves gelatine
400 ml / 13 ½ fl. oz / 1 ½ cups prune juice
1 tbsp tarragon leaves
6 cloves garlic
Handful mixed olives, stoned

495

SERVES 6

Chicken and Aubergine Saltimbocca

- Preheat the oven to 180°C / 350F / gas 5. Cut the aubergines (eggplants) into thin slices lengthways.
- Place on a lined baking tray and drizzle generously with oil. Season and cook for 20 minutes, turning half way through.
- Meanwhile cut the chicken in half lengthways.
- Heat a little oil in a pan and cook the chicken on both sides until golden. Season and drain on kitchen paper.
- Finely chop the basil and sage, then mix with oil in a pestle and mortar to form a paste. Season and set aside.
- Place 6 slices of aubergine (eggplant) on a baking sheet. Place a chicken slice on top and spread over some of the herb paste. Top with a slice of aubergine and repeat.
- Finish with a slice of rosemary tucked in then return to the oven for 15 minutes.
- Serve with roasted tomatoes.

PREPARATION TIME: 30 MINUTES

COOKING TIME: 35 MINUTES

....

INGREDIENTS

2 aubergines (eggplants)
6 chicken breasts, skinned
2 tbsp basil, chopped
2 sage leaves
3 cloves garlic
100 ml / 3 ½ fl. oz / ½ cup olive oil
6 sprigs rosemary

Chicken Saltimbocca with Balsamic

496

Drizzle with a little balsamic before serving.

497

SERVES 4

Veal and Mozzarella Saltimbocca

PREPARATION TIME: 10 MINUTES

COOKING TIME: 10 MINUTES

INGREDIENTS

4 slices rose veal escalope
1 ball mozzarella
4 slices Parma ham
4 sage leaves
4 cherry tomatoes, halved
3 slices stale white bread, made into breadcrumbs
2 tbsp plain (all purpose) flour
1 egg, beaten
2 tbsp olive oil

- Place the veal between 2 slices clingfilm (plastic wrap) and bat out with a rolling pin until very thin.
- Lay a slice of mozzarella, 2 tomato halves and a slice of Parma ham on top of the escalope and lightly press a sage leaf into the ham.
- Roll up the escalope and secure with a toothpick. Repeat for all the escalopes.
- Place the breadcrumbs, flour and egg on separate plates. Dunk the escalopes into the flour, then the egg then the breadcrumbs, coating on all sides. Season with salt and pepper.
- Heat the oil in a pan and when hot, add the escalopes and cook on all sides until golden brown and cooked through – approximately 10-12 minutes.
- Serve hot with a salad.

Saltimbocca with Gorgonzola

498

Use Gorgonzola instead of mozzarella.

499

SERVES 4

Breaded Stuffed Chicken

PREPARATION TIME: 20 MINUTES

COOKING TIME: 15 MINUTES

INGREDIENTS

4 chicken breast fillets
8 slices braesola (dry-cured beef)
1 ball mozzarella
1 tbsp rosemary leaves, finely chopped
5 tbsp olive oil

- Place the fillets between 2 sheets of clingfilm (plastric wrap) and bat out till quite thin.
- Lay over a slice of braesola then mozzarella slices and rosemary, then roll up and secure with a toothpick.
- Heat the oil in a pan and cook the escalopes on all sides until golden,
- Cover with a lid and cook for another 3 minutes until the chicken is cooked through.
- Serve hot.

Breaded Stuffed Chicken with Fontina

500

Use a Fontina instead of mozzarella

Breaded Stuffed Chicken with Tomatoes

501

Include sun blushed tomatoes in the stuffing

502

SERVES 6

Penne with Beef Stew

PREPARATION TIME 45 MINUTES

COOKING TIME 3 HOURS
30 MINUTES

....

INGREDIENTS

2 carrots, peeled
2 onions, peeled and chopped
3 cloves of garlic, peeled
zest of 1 orange
1 bouquet garni
600 g / 1 1 ⅓ lb / 2 ½ cups stewing beef, cubed
3 tbsp olive oil
500 ml / 1 pint / 2 cups red wine
2 cloves
125 g / 4 oz / ½ cup smoked bacon lardons
1 tbsp tomato puree
500 g / 1 lb / 2 cups penne pasta
salt and pepper

Penne with Pork Stew   503

Replace the beef with pork.

- Finely chop the carrots, 1 onion and 1 garlic clove in a food processor.
- Place in a bowl with the orange zest, bouquet garni and the meat. Pepper generously, add oil and the red wine. Cover and leave to marinate for 24 hours in the refrigerator.
- The same day, peel the remaining onion, cut in half and push the cloves into it.
- Remove the meat from the marinade, and add to a casserole in batches. Return all the meat to the pan.
- Add the lardons, garlic and onion and fry gently until the fat runs, and then stir in the tomato puree. Season and cook for 10 minutes.
- Add the marinade and its ingredients and turn up the heat until it's simmering. Cover and cook over the lowest heat for 3 hours.
- Cook the pasta according to packet instructions, and drain and toss when finished.
- Fish the clove-d onion and bouquet garni out of the stew and serve with the pasta.
-

504

SERVES 6

Rabbit Stew with Aubergine

PREPARATION TIME: 30 MINUTES

COOKING TIME:
1 HOUR 20 MINUTES

INGREDIENTS

4 tbsp olive oil
1 rabbit, jointed
1 tbsp tomato puree
1 sprig thyme
1 bay leaf
300 ml / 10 fl. oz / 1 ¼ cups white wine
400 g / 14 oz / 2 cups chopped tomatoes
2 tbsp chives, chopped
3 aubergines (eggplants), thinly sliced
1 tbsp olive oil
6 tomatoes, peeled and chopped
Pinch saffron

- Heat the oil tbsp oil in a casserole and brown the rabbit all over. Add the tomato puree and white wine along with the herbs, season with salt and pepper, cover and cook gently for 30 minutes.
- Near the end of the cooking time add the tomatoes and chives, then crumble in the saffron and cook for another 30 minutes.
- Meanwhile cook the aubergines (eggplants) in olive oil, turning carefully until golden and tender. Drain on kitchen paper.
- Cook the chopped tomatoes in the pan until just collapsing.
- Place the aubergine (eggplant) rounds on a plate and spoon over the tomato.
- Serve the rabbit on top.

Rabbit Stew with Red Pepper 505

Add 1 chopped red pepper to the stew with the rabbit.

506

SERVES 4

Mimolette and Chicken Panini

PREPARATION TIME: 5 MINUTES

COOKING TIME: 5 MINUTES

INGREDIENTS

4 panini rolls
2 tbsp oil
4 chicken fillets, skinned
½ lemon, juiced
8 slices Mimolette cheese
1 little gem lettuce, shredded

- Cook the Panini rolls according to packet instructions.
- Meanwhile bat out the chicken breasts in 2 pieces of clingfilm (plastic wrap) until thinner.
- Heat the oil in a pan and cook the chicken on both sides until golden. Season wth salt and pepper and squeeze over a little lemon juice.
- Slice the paninis open and layer on the lettuce, chicken and then the cheese.
- Grill until the cheese melts then serve.

Mimolette and Pesto Panini 507

Spread with a little pesto mixed with mayonnaise before adding the lettuce.

Mimolette and Prosciutto Panini 508

Add a slice of prosciutto on top of the chicken.

509

SERVES 4

Rabbit and Spring Vegetable Stew

- Heat the butter in a casserole pan with the oil then seal the rabbit in batches on all sides. Remove to a plate.
- Cook the onion in the butter until soft and translucent. Return the rabbit to the pan.
- Pour over the stock and add the thyme. Bring to a simmer then cook for 20 minutes over a low heat.
- Add the carrots and turnips and cook for a further 20 minutes.
- Add the peas and cook for 5 minutes.
- Season with salt and pepper. If the sauce is too liquid, remove the rabbit and vegetables and reduce to the desired consistency, then return them to the pan to heat through before serving.

PREPARATION TIME: 5 MINUTES

COOKING TIME: 1 HOUR

INGREDIENTS

1 rabbit, jointed
2 tbsp butter
2 tbsp olive oil
1 onion, finely chopped
500 ml / 1 pint / 2 cups chicken stock
1 sprig thyme
200 g / 7 oz carrots, scrubbed
8 baby turnips, scrubbed
200 g / 6 ½ oz / ¾ cup peas, frozen or fresh

510

SERVES 4

Chicken Saltimbocca

- Place the fillets in between 2 slices of clingfilm (plastic wrap) and bat out until very thin with a rolling pin.
- Cut the cheese into 8 slices.
- Lay a chicken escalope out on the surface, season it then place a slice of cheese and 3 basil leaves on top. Top this with a slice of ham and another slice of cheese.
- Roll the escalope up into a roulade and secure with a toothpick. Repeat for all the chicken slices.
- Heat the oil in a pan, then add the saltimbocca and garlic and cook until golden all over – about 10 minutes.
- Serve warm a salad.

PREPARATION TIME: 10 MINUTES

COOKING TIME: 10 MINUTES

INGREDIENTS

4 chicken fillets
250 g / 9 oz / 1 cup Cantal cheese
12 thin slices cured ham
12 basil leaves
4 tbsp olive oil

DESSERTS

Strawberry and Pistachio Tiramisu

Cherry and Pistachio Tiramisu

512

Swap the weight of strawberries for 350 g / 12 oz of cherries and cook the same

Strawberry and Banana Tiramisu

513

Swap the pistachio paste for 30 g / 1 oz of mashed banana for a fruity Tiramisu

Chocolate and Pistachio Tiramisu

514

Combine 350 g / 12 oz of melted chocolate with the sugar and continue the method.

PREPARATION TIME: 30 MINUTES

RESTING TIME: 3 HOURS

INGREDIENTS

500 g / 1 lb 2 oz / 2 cups of Mascarpone
125 g / 4 ½ oz / ½ cup of caster (superfine) sugar (⅘ for mascarpone and ⅕ for strawberries)
350 g / 12 oz / 1 ½ cups of strawberries
30 g / 1 oz of pistachio paste
6 egg yolks
250 ml / 8 fl. oz / 1 cup of whipping cream
20 finger biscuits
120 ml / 4 fl. oz / ½ cup of milk
Crushed pistachios and mint leaves for decoration

- Separate the eggs then mix the yolks and 100 g / 3 ½ oz of sugar till frothy.
- Add the Mascarpone and separate in 2 bowls.
- Whip the cream until stiff and add to the 2 mixtures.
- Blend half the strawberries with 25 g / 1 oz of sugar, then combine with one of the mascarpone mixtures. Combine the other mix with the pistachio paste.
- Soak the finger biscuits in the milk and line the bottom of the serving dishes with half of them.
- Top with Mascarpone mixture with pistachio, then half the remaining strawberries and the remaining biscuit.
- Top with the strawberry Mascarpone mixture and the rest of the strawberries, crushed pistachios and mint leaves. You can caramelize the pistachio for added crunch.
- Chill for 3 hours.

Panna Cotta with Hibiscus Syrup

515

SERVES 8

- Soak the gelatine powder in cold water.
- Heat the coconut milk, cream, half the sugar, and the vanilla pod sliced in half lengthwise on medium heat without boiling.
- Remove the mixture from the heat, drain to remove the vanilla pod then add the dissolved gelatine and stir.
- Pour the mixture into cone dishes, and refrigerate for about 4 hours or overnight.
- To shape the hibiscus flowers, cook the remaining sugar with the same amount of water until slightly golden, let cool a bit then dip the hibiscus flowers in the caramel and let set upside down (pegs can be used). Reserve the reamining syrup.
- Unmould the panacotta then top with the hibiscus flower and serve with the Hibiscus syrup.

PREPARATION TIME: 20 MINUTES

RESTING TIME: 4 HOURS

....

INGREDIENTS

350 ml / 12 fl. oz / 1 ½ cup coconut milk
250 ml / 8 fl. oz / 1 cup double cream
110 g / 4 oz / ½ cup caster (superfine) sugar
8 hibiscus flowers
100 ml / 3 ⅓ fl. oz / ½ cup hibiscus syrup
1 vanilla pod
5 g / ¼ oz gelatine powder

Panacotta with Strawberry Syrup

516

Replace the hibiscus syrup with strawberry coulis perfumed with rose water, and the hibiscus flower by rose petals

Italian Chocolate Ice Cream

517

SERVES 6

- Mix the evaporated milk with the milk in a saucepan and heat without boiling.
- Mix the sugar and egg yolk and pour the egg mixture gently into the hot milk mixture, stirring constantly. Cook for 10 minutes.
- Melt the chocolate over a Bain Marie then slowly incorporate the chocolate to the milk.
- Remove from the heat and let cool to room temperature.
- Add the yoghurt and mix well, then refrigerate.
- Churn for 40 minutes in an ice-cream maker or place in the freezer for 4 hours, whisking regularly until frozen.

PREPARATION TIME:
20 MINUTES

COOKING TIME : 20 MINUTES

....

INGREDIENTS

250 g / 9 fl. oz / 1 cup evaporated milk
250 ml / 9 fl. oz / 1 cup of milk
3 egg yolks
150 g / 5 oz full fat plain yoghurt
4 tbsb sugar
150 g / 5 oz of dark chocolate

Italian Strawberry Ice Cream

518

Replace the dark chocolate with 250 g / 9 oz of strawberries and 3 tablespoons of strawberry syrup.

519

MAKES 40

Italian Vanilla Cookies

PREPARATION TIME: 50 MINUTES

COOKING TIME: 10 MINUTES

INGREDIENTS

175 g / 6 oz / 2 / 3 cup plain (all purpose) flour
125 g / 4 ½ oz of salted butter, softened
75 g / 3 oz of sugar
1 egg yolk
1 tbsp Vanilla extract
Icing (confectioner's) sugar, for finishing

- Put the flour in a bowl. Form a well and add the diced butter, sugar and egg yolks. Work the dough quickly with your fingertips to get coarse crumbs.
- Add the Vanilla extract and work the dough, just enough to form a ball. Place it in film and keep it refrigerated for 30 minutes.
- Preheat the oven to 180°C / 350F / gas 4.
- Roll out the dough on a floured surface, or better yet, between two sheets of wax paper or plastic wrap to a thickness of about 7 mm / ¾ ".
- Using a pastry cutter, cut out round shapes then make a hole in the middle.
- Place the cookies on a non-stick baking tray and cook for 10 minutes. The cookies should remain light in colour and still very flexible in the oven.
- Remove them and cool them on a rack. When cool, sprinkle with icing sugar.

Lemon Cookies

Follow the above recipe, replacing the vanilla extract with the juice and zest of one lemon

520

521

SERVES 6

Raspberry Tiramisu

PREPARATION TIME: 20 MINUTES

COOKING TIME: 2 HOURS

INGREDIENTS

250 g / 9 oz of raspberries
500 g / 1 lb 2 oz of Mascarpone
110 g / 4 oz / ½ cup of caster (superfine) sugar
2 eggs, separated
12 finger biscuits
150 ml / 5 fl. oz / ½ cup of Marsala
Cocoa powder, to serve

- Mix the Mascarpone with the sugar and beaten eggs yolks.
- Whisk the egg whites to soft peaks and fold into the egg yolk mixture.
- Puree the raspberries and keep a few for decoration.
- Place the raspberry coulis at the bottom of the serving dishes.
- Dip the finger biscuits in Marsala and place them over the raspberry coulis.
- Add the Mascarpone mixture, then dust with cocoa powder.
- Finish with the fresh raspberries and chill for 2 hours.

Blueberry Tiramisu

Swap the amount of raspberries for blueberries.

522

523

SERVES 4

Rose-water Panna Cotta

Rose-water Panna Cotta with Berries

524

Replace the lychees with half raspberries and strawberries marinated with 1 tsp of sugar and 1 tbsp of lemon juice.

Coconut Panna Cotta

525

Use coconut cream instead of cream and almond milk instead of milk in equal quantities, and 1 tbsp of agar instead of gelatine.

PREPARATION TIME: 4 HOURS 20 MINUTES

COOKING TIME: 20 MINUTES

INGREDIENTS

250 ml / 8 fl. oz / 1 cup double (heavy) cream
1 tbsp milk
110 g / 4 oz / ½ cup caster (superfine) sugar
3 sheets gelatine
200 g / 7 oz / 1 cup lychees
2 tbsp rose water
Dried rose buds for decoration (optional)

- Put the gelatine in a bowl of cold water until it's softened, then drain and reserve.
- Lightly oil a tray of heart shaped (or any shaped) cake moulds.
- Heat the milk and cream in a saucepan with the sugar over low heat until the sugar is dissolved.
- Remove from the heat.
- Stir the gelatine into the milk-cream-sugar mixture, then add the rose water.
- Stir until the mixture is smooth and pour into the moulds and refrigerate for 4 hours, ideally overnight.
- Just before serving, unmold (dip the bottom of each mould in a bowl of hot water, and run a knife around for easy removal) on plates.
- Garnish with halved lychees and dried rose buds.

526

SERVES 6

Fig and Chocolate Focaccia

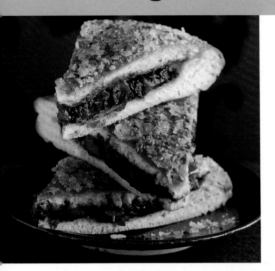

- To prepare the dough, combine in a bowl the flour, the white wine and olive oil, then the yeast and salt.
- Knead for 10 minutes and set aside covered with a dry cloth for 2 hours.
- Melt the chocolate over a Bain-Marie with 2 tbsp of cream. Chop the dried figs and mix them with the chocolate, then add the eggs.
- Whip the cream until stiff then gently fold with the slightly cooled chocolate and figs mixture. Reserve.
- Flatten the dough to about 1 cm / ½" and cut 2 circles.
- Place the first circle into a dish, top with the chocolate mixture, leaving the borders free. Top with the second circle of dough and press the borders together.
- Prick with a fork and score the dough, then bake for 30 minutes. Decorate the top with flaked almonds, grated coconut or chocolate sauce. Serve warm with ice cream.

PREPARATION TIME:
2 HOURS 20

COOKING TIME: 30 MINUTES

INGREDIENTS

FOR THE DOUGH
500 g / 1 lb 2 oz flour
1 tbsp baking powder
250 ml / 8 fl. oz / 1 cup of white wine
250 ml / 8 fl. oz / 1 cup of olive oil
a pinch of salt

FOR THE FILLING
250 g / 9 oz of dark chocolate
250 g / 9 oz of dried figs
2 eggs
250 ml / 8 fl. oz / 1 cup of cream

Bilberry Tiramisu

527

SERVES 4

PREPARATION TIME: 10 MINUTES

RESTING TIME: 3 HOURS

INGREDIENTS

4 Madeleine cakes
250 g / 9 oz of Mascarpone
120 ml / 4 fl. oz / ½ cup of double (heavy) cream

200 g / 7 oz of blueberries
3 egg yolks
110 g / 4 oz of caster (superfine) sugar
60 g / 2 ½ oz of poppy seeds
60 g / 2 ½ oz of brown sugar
A pinch of cinnamon
1 tbsp of Amaretto
4 tbsp of Marsala

- Mix the blueberries with sugar and cinnamon. Cool and refrigerate for 1 hour, stirring occasionally.
- In a bowl, whisk the Mascarpone with the egg yolks, sugar, poppy seeds and Amaretto.
- Add the cream after whipping it until stiff. Cool and refrigerate.
- Line the bottom of each glass with broken Madeleine soaked in Marsala.
- Place a first layer of mascarpone cream, then the blueberries with cinnamon.
- Cover with a second layer of cream.
- Sprinkle with poppy seeds and cinnamon powder.
- Cool and refrigerate for 2 hours before serving.

Amaretti

528

MAKES 40

PREPARATION TIME: 30 MINUTES

COOKING TIME: 30 MINUTES

INGREDIENTS

225 g / 8 oz / 2 cups ground almonds
150 g / 5 oz / 1 cup sifted icing (confectioner's) sugar
1 egg white

1 to 2 tbsp almond extract
Blanched almonds for decoration (optional)

- Preheat the oven to 180C (160C fan) / 350F / gas mark 4.
- Grease 2 baking trays and cover with baking paper.
- Whisk the egg white and almond extract in a bowl until frothy.
- Put the ground almonds and icing sugar in a large bowl and make a well.
- Add the egg white and mix with a metal spoon until the dough is a soft texture.
- Form into balls about a teaspoon worth of dough and arrange on the baking sheets, spacing them well. They can be decorated with a blanched almond each.
- Cook the biscuits for 15 to 20 minutes, they should be lightly browned.
- Let them cool on a rack.

529

SERVES 6

Tiramisu and Raspberry Sorbet

- Boil 2 / 3 of the Marsala and 200 ml / 7 fl. oz of water. Cool and filter.
- Whisk the mascarpone in a bowl with the crème fraiche, half the icing sugar and remaining Marsala.
- Mash half the raspberries with the remaining sugar then filter to get rid of the pips and get a smooth raspberry coulis.
- Dip the finger biscuits into the Marsala mixture.
- Place half the Mascarpone mixture in the serving dishes, then the finger biscuits and half the raspberry coulis.
- Top with the rest of the Mascarpone cream and the rest of the coulis. Sprinkle with the remaining raspberries.
- Put the tiramisu in the fridge for at least 4 hours.
- Serve well chilled with a scoop of raspberry sorbet and some mint leaves.

PREPARATION TIME:
4 HOURS 20 MINUTES

COOKING TIME: 10 MINUTES

INGREDIENTS

400 g / 14 oz of Mascarpone
500 ml / 1 pt of raspberry sorbet
400 g / 2 cups of raspberries
4 tbsp of crème fraiche
120 g / 5 oz of icing (confectioners') sugar
12 finger biscuits
150 ml / 5 fl. oz / 2 / 3 cup of Marsala
Water
6 mint leaves for decoration

Tiramisu and Lemon Sorbet

530

Replace the raspberry sorbet with lemon and for the topping use lemon zest.

531

SERVES 6

Fior di Latte with Liquorice

- Mix the milk, sugar, salt and vanilla sugar in a saucepan.
- Beat the egg white until stiff and incorporate into the previous mixture.
- Heat the mixture slowly until bubbling then remove from the heat.
- Beat the cream until stiff.
- Fold gently with the previous mixture when cool until smooth.
- Pour the mix into an ice-cream machine for 40 minutes, or place in the freezer for 4 hours, churning every 30 minutes until the ice-cream starts to stiffen.
- Serve with liquorice syrup.

PREPARATION TIME: 10 MINUTES
COOKING TIME: 10 MINUTES

FREEZING TIME:
40 MINUTES TO 4 HOURS

INGREDIENTS

450 ml / 1 pt of cream
60 ml / 2 fl. oz / ¼ cup of milk
100 g / 4 oz of icing (confectioner's) sugar
1 sachet of vanilla sugar
1 egg white
salt
liquorice syrup for serving

532
SERVES 6

Sicilian Cannoli with Ricotta

Lime Cannoli

533

For an extra zesty twist on this recipe, substitute the lemon with a lime.

PREPARATION TIME: 25 MINUTES

COOKING TIME: 35 MINUTES

INGREDIENTS

800 g / 1 lb 12 oz / 4 cups plain (all purpose) flour
150 g / 5oz / ⅔ cup butter
4 eggs
120 ml / 4 fl. oz / ½ cup white wine
75 g / 3 oz caster / ⅓ cup (superfine) sugar
Drop vanilla extract
250 g / 9 oz / 1 cup ricotta
250 g / 9 oz / 1 cup sugar
4 tbsp pistachio nuts, chopped
30 g / 1 oz dark chocolate, grated
4 tbsp orange peel, crystallised
3 l / 6 pts / 12 cups cooking oil
Pinch salt

- To prepare the cannoli place the flour on a work surface and dig a well in the centre.
- Incorporate the butter, sugar, white wine and eggs.
- Combine together into a smooth paste and let rest for about 1 hour.
- Spread the dough finely with a rolling pin and cut it into 10 cm / 4" disks.
- Wrap the dough discs on rolls coated with oil.
- Heat the oil in a fryer and immerse the cylinders holding the dough. Remove them as soon as they are golden.
- Let cool on paper towels then remove the dough cylinders.
- For the cream: whisk the ricotta with the sugar and when the mixture is well blended, add the grated chocolate with ¾ of the chopped crystallised orange peel and pistachios.
- Stuff the cannolli with the ricotta cream and sprinkle the ends with the rest of the orange and pistachios.

534

SERVES 6

Summer Fruit and Mascarpone

- Butter a 20 cm round pan.
- Wash the fruits.
- Sprinkle 1 tbsp of sugar over the fruit and reserve.
- Pre-heat the oven at 180°C (160°F) / 350F / gas 6.
- In a small saucepan over very low heat, melt the butter, then remove from the heat.
- Add the sugar and mix until blended.
- Add the two eggs, mix again, then add the mascarpone.
- Finish mixing with 60 g of flour and 1 tbsp of amaretto.
- Place the fruits in the dish then spread the cream over the fruit.
- Cook for 25 minutes then let cool and serve with vanilla ice cream.

PREPARATION TIME: 20 MINUTES

COOKING TIME: 25 MINUTES

INGREDIENTS

600 g / 1 ⅓ lb summer fruits: raspberries, strawberries, blueberries, redcurrants
200 g / 7 oz mascarpone
100 g / 4 oz / 1 stick of butter
75 g / 3 oz sugar
60 g / 2 ½ oz flour
2 eggs
1 tbsp of amaretto

Autumn Mascarpone Gratin   535

Replace the summer fruits by the same quantity of a mix of apples, pears and cooked chestnuts.

536

SERVES 6

Struffoli

- Mix the sugar with egg until the mixture is frothy.
- Place the flour in a bowl and make a well. Add the egg mixture, butter slightly melted, vanilla pod seeds and a pinch of salt.
- Add the liqueur and work the dough again.
- Flour the work surface and form small balls of different sizes.
- Heat the oil for frying. Place the small balls in hot oil and let them cook until they are golden brown. Then remove the Struffoli and place them on absorbent paper.
- Meanwhile, melt the honey over low heat. Simmer, until the honey is very liquid.
- Drop the Struffoli in honey. Mix thoroughly so that all balls are coated with honey.
- Place the Struffoli in a dish and let cool overnight if possible.
- Decorate with candied fruits or sprinkles.

PREPARATION TIME: 30 MINUTES

COOKING TIME: 10 MINUTES

RESTING TIME: 12 HOURS

INGREDIENTS

450 g / 1 lb / 2 cups plain (all purpose) flour
2 tbsp sugar
2 tbsp butter
4 eggs
Pinch salt
2 vanilla pods
2 tbsp Amaretto liqueur
5 tbsp honey
Vegetable oil, for frying

Aniseed and Lemon Zest Struffoli   537

Incorporate the zest of 2 lemons into the dough, as well as 2 teaspoons of aniseed.

538

SERVES 6

Profiteroles

PREPARATION TIME: 45 MINUTES

COOKING TIME: 45 MINUTES

INGREDIENTS

FOR THE CHOUX PASTRY
150 g / 5 oz / 1 cup plain (all purpose) flour
125 g / 4 ½ oz / ½ cup butter
4 eggs
1 tbsp sugar
2 pinches salt

FOR THE SAUCE
150 g / 5 oz / ½ cup dark chocolate
2 tbsp butter
1 tablespoon milk

FOR THE FILLING
250 ml / 8 fl. oz / 1 cup double (heavy) cream
25 g / 1 oz icing (confectioner's) sugar

- Preheat the oven to 210°C / 420F / gas 7.
- Heat the butter over low heat then add the sugar, salt and 250 ml / 8 fl. oz / 1 cup of water and whisk.
- Remove from the heat and add the flour all at once, whisking. Return to the heat and cook, stirring quickly until the dough pulls away from pan.
- Remove the pan from the heat and stir in the eggs one at a time, while still whisking.
- Place the dough in a piping bag fitted with a plain tip and form small balls of dough on a baking sheet, spacing them well as they rise during cooking.
- Bake for 30 minutes, leaving the door slightly open to let the moisture escape.
- Break the chocolate in a saucepan. Add the butter in pieces and milk. Melt over low heat, stirring until you obtain a sauce. Reserve in a water bath.
- Beat the cream until stiff then incorporate the sugar and refrigerate.
- Remove the choux from the oven and let cool.
- Cut the choux three-quarters of their height. Fill each with a small scoop of whipped cream. Place the caps on top.
- Place the choux in bowls and sprinkle with chocolate sauce. Serve immediately.

539

MAKES 20

Fig and Almond Panetti

PREPARATION TIME: 10 HOURS

COOKING TIME: 1 HOUR

INGREDIENTS

700 g / 1 lb 8 oz / 3 cups plain (all purpose) flour
700 g / 1 lb 8 oz / 3 cups honey
400 g / 13 oz / 2 cups dark chocolate
1 ½ tbsp cocoa powder
450 g / 1 lb / 2 cups peanuts
250 g / 9 oz / 1 cup almonds
200 g / 7 oz / 1 cup hazelnuts (cob nuts)
50 g / 2 oz of dried figs
120 ml / 4 fl. oz / ½ cup olive oil
1 tbsp black pepper
Nutmeg, grated to taste

- Pour the honey into a pan with the chocolate cut into pieces
- Dissolve the honey and chocolate over low heat, stirring occasionally.
- Cut the figs into small pieces, hazelnuts (cob nuts) and almonds in half and leave the whole peanuts.
- Put the flour in a bowl, pour the melted chocolate and honey and mix. Pour the oil and mix again.
- Add all the dried fruit, grated nutmeg, pepper and cocoa.
- Mix all the ingredients by hand.
- Make dough balls and place them carefully on the baking sheet, spaced enough from each other.
- Rest for 10 hours if possible.
- Cook the dough at 150°C / 300F / gas 2 for about one hour, checking frequently.
- Eat slightly warm.

Fig and Pine Nut Panetti

540

Swap the 250 g almonds for 250 g of pine nuts.

541

MAKES 18

Cappuccino Cream Dessert

Pistachio Cream Dessert

 542

Replace the cappuccino mix and chocolate with 60 g / 1 oz of pistachio paste, and sprinkle with chopped pistachios instead of chocolate sauce.

Coffee and Almond Dessert

543

Replace the Cappuccino with 25 g / 1 oz of instant coffee and the cocoa with 40 g / 1 ½ oz of almond powder. Sprinkle with chopped almonds.

PREPARATION TIME:
15 MINUTES

COOKING TIME: 15 MINUTES

RESTING TIME : 30 MINUTES

INGREDIENTS

1 litre / 2 pts milk
125 g / 4 ½ oz sugar
50 g / 2 oz cornstarch
50 g / 2 oz Cappuccino powder mix
25 g / 1 oz unsweetened bitter cocoa
30 cl / 10 fl. oz liquid whipping cream
1 tbsb icing (confectioner's) sugar
chocolate sauce
mozzarella
basil, to garnish

- Mix all the powders (cornstarch, sugar, unsweetened cocoa mixture and Cappuccino) with cold milk.
- Bring to a boil in a heavy saucepan and let thicken, stirring to prevent the bottom of the cream burning.
- Once the desired consistency of the cream is reached (usually just before boiling), remove from the heat and add half the cream.
- Leave cool to room temperature for about 30 minutes, stirring occasionally.
- Meanwhile, whisk the rest of the cream until stiff then add the icing sugar and whisk a bit more.
- Place the cream in pretty cups, and top with Chantilly cream with a piping bag and a sprinkle of chocolate sauce

544
SERVES 6
Pipasena Italian Cake

- Pre-heat the oven to 190°C (170° fan) / 375F / gas 5.
- Mix the raisins, candied fruits, rum and a little water in a bowl to marinate them.
- Heat in the microwave oven for 1 minute and let cool.
- Grate the zest of lemon.
- Heat the milk and butter until the butter is melted.
- Mix the flour and baking powder, add the eggs, then the warmed milk mixture .
- Add the sugar, vanilla sugar and oil.
- Fold in the grated zest and drained fruits and raisins gently.
- Cook for 40 minutes.

PREPARATION TIME: 20 MINUTES

COOKING TIME: 40 MINUTES

INGREDIENTS

450 g / 1 lb flour
200 g / 7 oz sugar
25 cl / 8 fl. oz / 1 cup of milk
125 g / 4 ½ oz butter
2 eggs
125 g / 4 ½ oz raisins
125 g / 4 ½ oz candied fruits
1 lemon
2 tbsp dark rum
1 tsp baking powder
1 sachet of vanilla sugar
3 tbsp oil

Bitter Chocolate Panna Cotta

545
SERVES 6

PREPARATION TIME: 5 HOURS

COOKING TIME: 35 MINUTES

INGREDIENTS

FOR THE PANACOTTA
150 g / 5 oz / ½ cup dark chocolate
750 ml / 1 ½ pints / 3 cups whipping cream

2 tbsp caster (superfine) sugar
4 gelatine sheets

FOR THE ORANGE MARMALADE
2 kg / 4 lbs juicy oranges
1 kg / 2 lbs jam sugar

- Wash the oranges, pricking them with a fork, putting them in cold water for 12 hours. Soak the gelatine in cold water.
- Heat the cream. Add the chocolate broken into pieces, the cream and the sugar. Stir constantly until chocolate is melted. Continue stirring until the mixture boils then remove from the heat.
- Stir in the gelatine leaves and whisk until melted. Pour into small individual dishes and refrigerate for 2 to 3 hours. For the marmalade, drain the oranges and discard the juice.
- Peel and keep the peel of 3 oranges only. Cut the peel into thin strips, and soak it for 3 to 4 minutes in boiling water.
- Peel the other oranges and slice into segments. Weigh them, put them in a pan with the same weight in sugar.
- Bring to a boil over medium heat. Simmer gently, without adding water and stir often.
- Add the strips of zest. Cook for 2 to 3 minutes, still stirring.
- Pour the hot jam into jars. Close immediately and let cool. To serve the panna cotta, unmould it and sprinkle with cooled orange marmalade.

Italian Rice Tart

546
SERVES 8

PREPARATION TIME:
10-15 MINUTES

COOKING TIME:
1 HOUR 20-25 MINUTES

INGREDIENTS

200 g / 7 oz / 1 cup arborio rice
450 ml / 16 fl. oz / 2 cups whole milk

450 g / 1 lb / 2 cups caster (superfine) sugar
450 g / 1 lb / 2 cups ricotta, drained
7 large eggs
110 g / 4 oz / ½ cup hazelnuts (cob nuts), roughly chopped
½ lemon, juiced
2 tsp vanilla extract

- Combine the rice and milk in a saucepan and cook until it starts to boil.
- Reduce the heat to very low and cook the rice uncovered for 15-20 minutes, until the rice has absorbed the milk and is sticky.
- Remove from the heat and set it to one side.
- Beat the eggs and sugar together in a bowl until they are well combined and the sugar has dissolved.
- Add the lemon juice and vanilla extract and stir. Combine the ricotta and rice until smooth.
- Fold this mixture into the eggs and sugar. Fold the hazelnut into the mixture.
- Preheat the oven to 180°C (160° fan) / 350F / gas 4.
- Grease and line a 7" cake tin with greaseproof paper.
- Spoon the mixture into the cake tin and bake for 50 minutes until the tart is puffed and brown in colour.
- Remove from the oven and let the tart cool.

547

SERVES 8

Semifreddo with Pastis

- In a pan over low heat mix the eggs and sugar for 5 minutes until the mixture is thickened.
- Remove from the heat and let cool.
- In a bowl whisk the cream into a Chantilly until stiff then incorporate to the cooled egg mixture.
- Add the Pastis and grated coconut.
- Place the mixture in glasses and freeze for at least 4 hours.
- Remove from the freezer about 15 minutes before serving.

PREPARATION TIME: 20 MINUTES
COOKING TIME: 10 MINUTES
FREEZING TIME: 4 HOURS

INGREDIENTS

450 ml / 16 fl. oz / 2 cups of cream
4 eggs
50 g / 2 oz of sugar
3 tablespoons of Pastis
2 tablespoons of grated coconut

Pistachio and Pomegranate Semifreddo

548

Replace the Pastis with pistachio extract or paste, and the coconut with 3 tbsp of pomegranate seeds.

549

SERVES 6

Chocolate Salamis

- Crumble the biscuits into small pieces.
- Beat 2 eggs with the sugar.
- Melt the butter and chocolate in a saucepan.
- Pour the melted chocolate over the beaten eggs, then stir in gradually the cookie pieces and the pine nuts.
- Mix everything evenly.
- Have a flat sheet of aluminum foil covered with a transparent plastic film of the same size.
- Pour the mixture into an elongated sausage shape (the aluminum foil will help solidify the resulting shape and the film will prevent the aluminum pieces to be embedded in the salami).
- Leave in a fridge for at least 24 hours.

PREPARATION TIME 20 MINS
COOKING TIME 10 MINS

INGREDIENTS

200 g / 7 oz / 1 cup butter biscuits
100 g / 3 ½ oz / ½ cup pine nuts
100 g / 3 ½ oz / ½ cup butter
100 g / 3 ½ oz / ½ cup dark chocolate
2 tbsp caster (superfine) sugar
2 eggs

Colourful Chocolate Salami

550

Replace the pine nuts with blanched pistachios and incorporate freeze-dried raspberries for a colourful twist.

551

SERVES 4

Ricotta Cake

Apple and Chocolate Ricotta Cake

552

follow the recipe but add 75 g / 3 oz of chocolate, broken into pieces, and 3 apples, peeled and diced, to the dough before cooking.

PREPARATION TIME: 15 MINUTES

COOKING TIME: 50 MINUTES

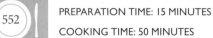

INGREDIENTS

250 g / 9 oz of ricotta
150 g / 5 oz of caster (superfine) sugar
150 g / 5 oz of plain (all purpose) flour
3 eggs
60 ml / 2 fl. oz / ¼ cup of milk
1 lemon, grated zest and juiced
Pinch powdered ginger

- Pre-heat the oven to 200°C (180° fan) / 400F / gas th.6.
- Put in the bowl the ricotta, eggs, sugar and ginger. Whip the cream until smooth.
- Add the grated lemon zest and juice, beat again.
- Add the flour gradually.
- Pour the batter into a buttered and floured pan.
- Cook in the oven for 30 to 40 minutes: the cake should be puffed and golden.
- Serve warm or cold.

553

SERVES 4

Rhubarb Tiramisu

- To prepare the mascarpone cream, mix the egg yolk, sugar and Mascarpone and stir in the egg white, after beating it until stiff. Chill.
- Wash and chop the rhubarb stalks. Cook them with the sugar in a covered pan over low heat, stirring occasionally with a wooden spoon. Reserve.
- Prepare the base by blending 150 g / 5 oz of cinnamon biscuits and combining it with the softened butter.
- Place the biscuit base in serving dishes, then half the Mascarpone cream and the rhubarb compote.
- Crumble a couple of biscuits on top of the rhubarb, then the rest of the Mascarpone cream.
- Chill in the fridge for at least 4 hours.
- Just before serving, the dishes can be sprinkled with cocoa powder, crumbled biscuits or a pinch of cinnamon powder.

PREPARATION TIME:
4 HOURS 15 MINUTES

COOKING TIME: 15 MINUTES

....

INGREDIENTS

For the Mascarpone cream
200 g / 7 oz of Mascarpone
100 g / 4 oz of caster (superfine) sugar
1 egg, separated

FOR THE RHUBARB COMPOTE
5 large stalks of rhubarb
110 g / 4 oz of brown sugar

FOR THE BASE
110 g / 4 oz / 1 stick of butter
200 g of cinnamon finger biscuits

554

SERVES 6

Raspberry and Champagne Zabaglione

- Put the eggs in a saucepan. Place the saucepan over a water bath, on a medium heat.
- Add the sugar, vanilla and lemon zest. Whisk until foamy and pale.
- Put the saucepan into a water bath on medium heat.
- Then stir in the Champagne gradually while beating.
- Puree the raspberries and filter to remove the pips.
- Add to the mixture and fold gently.
- Serve the warm zabaglione with almond biscuits or gingerbread.

PREPARATION TIME: 15 MINUTES

COOKING TIME: 15 MINUTES

....

INGREDIENTS

200 g / 7 oz / ¾ cup raspberries
180 g / 6 oz / 2 / 3 cup caster (superfine) sugar
400 ml / 13 fl. oz / 2 cups Champagne
8 egg yolks
1 tsp vanilla extract
1 lemon, grated zest and juiced

Chocolate and Champagne Zabaglione

555

Use 200 g / 7 oz / of melted chocolate rather than the raspberry and continue the method.

556

MAKES 10

Polenta and Chocolate Chip Cookies

PREPARATION TIME: 15 MINS

COOKING TIME: 15 MINS

....

INGREDIENTS

1 egg
3 tsp brown sugar
3 tsp butter
2 tbsp instant polenta
2 tbsp plain (all purpose) flour
½ tsp baking powder
2 tbsp chocolate chips

- Preheat the oven to 180°C / 350F / gas 4.
- In a bowl, whisk the egg with the sugar then add the butter and mix well.
- Add the polenta (without cooking it before), flour and baking powder.
- Once the mixture is smooth, take a tablespoon of dough, quickly forming a ball with your fingers and place on a baking sheet. Flatten with a spoon to form the cookie.
- Space the cookies well on the sheet.
- Cook for 15 minutes, then add the chocolate chips (they should stick to the cookies but not melt).
- Remove from the oven and transfer to a wire rack to cool.

Chocolate Orange Polenta Cookies

557

Add some orange peel in the mix for extra flavour, or some orange water.

558

SERVES 6

Strawberry Zabaglione

PREPARATION TIME: 40 MINS

COOKING TIME: 5 MINS

....

INGREDIENTS

500 g / 1 lb / 2 cups strawberries
150 g / 5 oz / 2 / 3 cup caster (superfine) sugar
100 g / 4 oz / ½ cup honey
125 g / 4 ½ oz / ½ cup Mascarpone
1 lemon
3 eggs
1 tsp cardamom seeds
100 ml / 3 ½ oz / ½ cup double (heavy) cream
2 tbsp white balsamic vinegar
250 ml / 8 fl. oz / 1 cup water
6 mint leaves

- Wash and hull the strawberries and cut them in two. Mix them with the juice of half the lemon and a tablespoon of caster sugar and reserve.
- Boil half the remaining sugar, water, vinegar and half the cardamom seeds to make a syrup.
- In another saucepan, caramelize the honey with the remaining cardamom and zest of lemon.
- Mix the flavoured honey with the syrup, then refrigerate. After cooling, filter and sprinkle half the strawberries and marinate for twenty minutes. Reserve.
- Break the eggs, add the remaining sugar and beat until white and compact. Beat the cream until stiff, mix with the cheese and add to the previous mixture.
- Arrange the fruit in syrup at the bottom of the serving dishes and top with the Mascarpone cream.
- Finish with the remaining strawberries and fresh mint leaves for serving.

Strawberry and Marshmallow Zabaglione

559

Top with marshmallows as a sweet, light alternative.

Gingerbread and Orange Tiramisu

560 SERVES 6

- Preheat the oven to 180°C (160°C fan) / 350F / gas 4.
- Grease a tin and line with greaseproof paper. Sift together the flour and ground ginger.
- Whisk the butter and sugar until fluffy. Beat in the honey and golden syrup and mix 2 tbsp of the flour mixture and beat the egg in.
- Fold in the flour, then follow with the milk. Spoon into the tin and bake for 45 minutes. Combine the water and sugar in a pan and cook over a low heat.
- Simmer for 5 minutes before adding the orange and cook for 10 minutes. Arrange on a baking tray. Remove the gingerbread and let it cool, then slice into triangles.
- Combine the cream, mascarpone, Marsala and sugar in a bowl and whisk. Spread the cream into the base of a glass dish. Arrange the triangles on top. Sprinkle the top with the cocoa powder.

PREPARATION TIME: 15 MINUTES
COOKING TIME: 1 HOUR
INGREDIENTS
300 g / 10 ½ oz / 2 cups plain flour
160 g / 5 ½ oz / 1 ½ sticks butter
75 g / 3 oz / ⅓ cup golden caster sugar
110 g / 4 oz / ⅓ cup golden syrup
125 g / 4 ½ oz / ½ cup honey
1 large egg
175 ml / 6 fl. oz / ¾ cup milk
1 ½ tsp ground ginger
500 ml / 1 pint / 2 cups whipping cream
250 g / 9 oz / 1 cup mascarpone
75 ml / 3 fl. oz / ⅓ cup Marsala
75 g / 3 oz / ⅓ cup caster sugar
1 orange, diced into small chunks
225 g / 8 oz / 1 cup caster sugar
250 ml / 9 fl. oz / 1 cup cold water

Grapefruit and Aniseed Tiramisu

561 SERVES 6

PREPARATION TIME: 30 MINUTES

RESTING TIME: 8 HOURS

INGREDIENTS

2 grapefruits
250 g / 9 oz of Mascarpone
110 g / 4 oz of sweetened condensed milk
90 g / 3 ½ oz of icing (confectioners') sugar
60 g / 2 ½ oz of ground almonds
60 g / 2 ½ oz of butter, melted
25 g / 1 oz of plain (all purpose) flour
4 egg whites
1 tbsp of icing (confectioners') sugar
1 tsp of aniseed extract
Vanilla pod for decoration

- Mix the Mascarpone with condensed milk. Reserve. Beat the egg whites until stiff and tighten them with icing sugar. Remove the zest from a grapefruit.
- Fold in half the egg whites with the Mascarpone, and gradually incorporating the grapefruit zest. Chill for at least 4 hours.
- Meanwhile, mix the flour, ground almonds, aniseed and icing sugar.
- Add the rest of the egg white gradually. Finish by adding the melted butter. Pour into a baking tray and bake at 170 °C / 350°F / gas 4 for 15 minutes. Let cool.
- Cut the grapefruit into segments.
- Line the serving dishes with the crumbled cake, then cover with half the mascarpone cream.
- Top with the grapefruit Supremes then the rest of Mascarpone cream and decorate with vanilla pod strips.

Polenta and Apricot Pudding

562 SERVES 4

PREPARATION TIME: 15 MINUTES

COOKING TIME: 15 MINUTES

RESTING TIME: 2 HOURS

INGREDIENTS

1 litre / 2 pts of milk
100 g / 4 oz of polenta
75 g / 3 oz of sugar
4 tbsp double cream
2 tbsp honey
1 tbsp cardamom
3 Gelatin leaves
a vanilla pod
a cinnamon stick
a pinch of cloves powder
½ tsp caster sugar
350 g / 12 oz / 1 ½ cup sliced
basil, to garnish

- Soak the gelatin leaves in a cold bowl of water.
- Wash and halve the apricots. Simmer them with a third of the vanilla pod and a tablespoon of sugar until tender but still holding (10 to 15 minutes)
- Pour the milk into a saucepan, immerse the remaining vanilla pod and cinnamon stick. Heat.
- Add the cardamom and clove powder, then the honey, remaining sugar and polenta and simmer about 10 minutes stirring continuously. After 5 minutes, remove the vanilla bean and cinnamon stick.
- Stir in the double cream then remove from the heat and add the drained gelatin and stir until dissolved.
- Place the halved apricots at the bottom of a ring mould, then pour the milk and polenta mixture and place in the refrigerator to set for at least 2 hours. Unmould and serve.

563

SERVES 6

Cherry Mascarpone Ice Cream

PREPARATION TIME: 20 MINUTES

FREEZING TIME : 6 HOURS

....

INGREDIENTS

250 ml / 8 fl. oz / 1 cup double cream
400 g / 13 oz mascarpone
250 ml / 8 fl. oz / 1 cup cane sugar
syrup
25 preserved cherries
cherry syrup
basil, to garnish

- Whip the cream until very stiff (but not churned).
- Whisk the mascarpone with the sugar cane syrup.
- Fold in the whipped cream and then gently the preserved cherries.
- Pour into a silicone cake mold and cover with plastic wrap.
- Press down well and freeze for at least 6 hours.
- Unmold, slice and serve with cherry syrup.

Mascarpone and Peach

564

For an extra zesty twist on this recipe, substitute the lemon with a lime.

565

SERVES 4

Melon Tiramisu

PREPARATION TIME 10 MINS

COOKING TIME 45 MINS

....

INGREDIENTS

1 Cantaloupe melon
10 finger biscuits
500 g / 1 lb 2 oz of Mascarpone
350 ml / 12 fl. oz / 1 ½ cup of double (heavy) cream
200 g / 7 oz of fresh pineapple
150 g / 5 oz of caster (superfine) sugar
3 tbsp of grated coconut
120 ml / 4 fl. oz / ½ cup of coconut milk
1 tsp of cinnamon powder

- Cut the melon in four, remove the skin and seeds and cut into thin strips.
- Cut the pineapple into very small dices.
- Whip the cream until stiff, then add the Mascarpone, sugar and coconut milk and continue to whisk until the mixture is homogeneous (do not overbeat).
- Coarsely crush the finger biscuits, and arrange them in the bottom of a dish.
- Sprinkle with coconut milk and a pinch of cinnamon.
- Cover with half of the cream, then the melon and pineapple and the remaining cream.
- Sprinkle with grated coconut and chill for at least 1 hour before serving.
- Finish with cinnamon powder.

Melon and Mango Tiramisu

566

Half the quantity of the melon and replace with the mango as a fruity treat.

567
SERVES 8 Semifreddo

- In a pan over low heat mix the eggs, egg yolks, sugar and vanilla for 5 minutes until the mixture is thickened.
- Remove from the heat and let cool.
- In a bowl whisk the cream until stiff then incorporate to the cooled egg mixture.
- Add the Cointreau and orange zest.
- Place the mixture in glasses and freeze for at least 4 hours.
- Remove from the freezer about 15 minutes before serving (the mixture needs to start melting slightly)
- Serve with chocolate pearls, orange zest or caramel shards.

PREPARATION TIME: 20 MINUTES

COOKING TIME: 10 MINUTES

FREEZING TIME: 8 HOURS

INGREDIENTS

450 ml / 16 fl. oz / 2 cups cream
3 eggs and 4 egg yolks
2 tbsp vanilla extract
4 tbsp sugar
4 tbsp Cointreau liqueur
1 tbsp orange zest

568
SERVES 4 Grilled Tutti Frutti Zabaglione

- Wash the fruits carefully. Hull the strawberries and currants. Cut the strawberries into two.
- In a bowl, beat the egg yolks with the champagne, then add the caster (superfine) sugar and whisk vigorously.
- When the mixture is fluffy, place in a water bath while continuing to whisk to incorporate air.
- When the zabaglione becomes denser, remove it from the water bath and continue to whisk until cool.
- Whip the cream with the icing (confectioners') sugar until stiff.
- Then combine the two mixtures, and refrigerate for 1 hour.
- Before serving, slice the rest of the fruits, place ¾ of the zabaglione in serving dishes, cover with fruits then top with the rest of the zabaglione and caramelize with a blowtorch or under the grill with a sprinkle of sugar.

PREPARATION TIME:
1 HOUR 15 MINUTES

COOKING TIME: 10 MINUTES

INGREDIENTS

2 kiwis
1 mango
2 bananas
100 g / 4 oz / ½ cup cherries
100 g / 4 oz / ½ cup blueberries
100 g / 4 oz / ½ cup strawberries
6 egg yolks
75 g / 3 oz / ⅓ cup caster (superfine) sugar
120 ml / 4 fl. oz / ½ cup double (heavy) cream
25 g / 1 oz icing (confectioners') sugar
60 ml / 2 fl. oz / ¼ cup of Champagne

Grilled Tropical Zabaglione

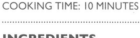

569

Replace the Champagne with Marsala and theme the fruits : tropical (passion fruit, pineapple, mango, banana, kiwi, grated coconut…).

570

SERVES 4

Sienna Nougat with Fruit

Walnuts and Chestnuts Nougat

571

Replace in equal quantities the hazelnuts with walnuts and the blanched almonds by candied chestnuts.

PREPARATION TIME: 10 MINUTES

COOKING TIME: 90 MINUTES

RESTING TIME : 60 MINUTES

....

INGREDIENTS

350 g / 12 oz blanched almonds
250 g / 9 oz liquid honey
225 g / 8 oz / 1 cup of sugar
200 g / 7 oz hazelnuts
3 egg whites
1 lemon and its zest
25 cl / 8 fl. oz / 1 cup of cream
1 tbs icing (confectioner's) sugar
100 g / 4 oz / ½ cup redcurrants
100 g / 4 oz / ½ cup raspberries
mint leaves

- Place the honey in a bowl over a Bain Marie and simmer for 10 minutes stirring regularly.
- Meanwhile, pre-heat the oven to 200°C (180°C fan) / 400F / gas 6.
- Grill the almonds and hazelnuts for 1 minute, checking regularly to ensure they don't burn. Reserve.
- In a pan make a caramel with the sugar and 100 ml / 3 fl. oz of water.
- Beat the egg whites until stiff then incorporate gently in the honey mixture.
- Add the caramel and mix thoroughly for 5 minutes.
- Add the hazelnuts, almonds, lemon zest and juice.
- Pour the mixture on a rectangular tray lined with baking paper.
- Level the mixture and cover with another baking paper.
- Let cool for up to an hour then cut into small squares. The nougat can be kept in an airtight container.
- To serve, beat the cream and incorporate the icing sugar. Top the nougat squares with the Chantilly, the washed redcurrants, raspberries and the mint leaves.

572

SERVES 6

Zuppa Inglese

- Heat ¾ of the milk, ¼ of the sugar and the chocolate until completely melted, then incorporate the cornstarch and cook until the mixture thickens.
- Let the mixture cool, stirring occasionally, then incorporate the coffee and stir.
- Pre-heat the oven to 180°C (160°C fan) / 350F / gas 4.
- Meanwhile, cut the brioche and soak it in a mix of the remaining milk, 1 egg and 3 egg yolks.
- Place half the soaked brioche in the bottom of a buttered dish, then top with the chocolate / coffee cream then with the rest of the brioche.
- Cook for 15 minutes, until the brioche firms up. Meanwhile, beat the remaining 3 egg whites until very stiff, then add the remaining sugar and beat again until the sugar is dissolved.
- Let the cake cool down, then cover with the egg white mixture and place in the oven for 5 minutes under the grill. The meringue should just start to brown.

Strawberry Zuppa Inglese

573

Replace the dark chocolate and coffee with 250 g / 9 oz strawberry puree: cook the soaked brioche on its own, then assemble with the cream containing the strawberry puree and the halved remaining strawberries.

PREPARATION TIME:
30 MINUTES

COOKING TIME: 30 MINUTES

INGREDIENTS

250 g / 9 oz Plain Panettone or brioche
4 eggs
100 g / 4 oz sugar
500 ml / 1 pt / 2 cups whole milk
75 g / 3 oz cornstarch
125 g / 4 ½ oz dark chocolate
1 tsp of instant coffee

574

SERVES 4

Risotto with Strawberries

- Place the rice, water, salt and butter in a saucepan and bring to the boil.
- Reduce to a simmer and let the rice absorb the water, stirring occasionally, until all of it has been absorbed.
- Meanwhile, combine the milk and caster sugar together in a separate saucepan.
- Bring to a simmer over a medium heat then add to the rice once it has absorbed all the water.
- Cook over a low heat for 10-15 minutes, stirring occasionally, until rich and thick.
- Add the strawberry halves and stir gently.
- Spoon into serving bowls and garnish with the freshly ground black pepper before serving.

PREPARATION TIME:
10-15 MINUTES

COOKING TIME: 25-30 MINUTES

INGREDIENTS

350 g / 12 oz / 3 cups strawberries, hulled and halved
110 g / 4 oz / ½ cup risotto rice
250 ml / 9 fl. oz / 1 cup water
250 ml / 9 fl. oz / 1 cup semi-skimmed milk
110 g / 4 oz / ½ cup caster (superfine) sugar
1 tbsp unsalted butter
a pinch of salt
freshly ground black pepper

575

SERVES 8

Panacotta with Raspberries

PREPARATION TIME:
5 HOURS 20 MINUTES

COOKING TIME: 10 MINUTES

INGREDIENTS

1 1/2 pts / 4 cups whipping cream
110 g / 4 oz / ½ cup sugar
3 gelatine sheets
1 vanilla pod

FOR THE COULIS AND SERVING
500 g / 1 lb 2 oz / 2 cups raspberries
200 g / 7 oz / 1 cup sugar
8 mint leaves, for decoration

- Soak the gelatine in cold water, drain and reserve.
- Boil the cream with the sugar and vanilla pod cut in its length.
- Turn off the heat and add the gelatine, stirring.
- Strain the cream and let it cool, stirring often.
- Pour the cream into the serving dishes or glasses and keep in the fridge for 5 hours.
- Prepare the coulis by mixing the cleaned raspberries (minus a handful for decoration) and the sugar. Keep in the fridge.
- Before serving, unmold the panacotta or serve it in its pretty glass with the raspberry coulis and fresh raspberries and mint leaves.

576

SERVES 8

Panettone

PREPARATION TIME: I HOUR

COOKING TIME: 50 MINUTES

INGREDIENTS

450 g / 1 lb / 2 cups strong white bread flour
extra flour, for dusting
225 g / 8 oz / 2 sticks butter
110 g / 4 oz / ½ cups caster (superfine) sugar
110 g / 4 oz / 2 / 3 cup candied peel
1 tsp vanilla extract
2 medium eggs
5 medium egg yolks
1 medium egg white
grated zest of 1 orange
grated zest of 1 lemon
30 g / 1 oz / 2 tbsp fresh yeast
30 ml / 1 fl. oz / 2 tbsp whole milk
75 g / 3 oz / ⅓ cup raisins
75 g / 3 oz / ⅓ cup sultanas
1 tsp salt
1 / 4 tsp freshly ground nutmeg
1 tsp icing sugar, for dusting

- Whisk the eggs, egg yolks and vanilla extract together in a bowl. In a separate bowl, beat together the butter and all but 1 tbsp of the caster sugar for 4-5 minutes.
- Add the beaten egg mixture to the butter and sugar, beating all the time. Heat the milk then crumble the yeast on top and add 1 tbsp of caster sugar. Leave to activate and froth.
- Sift the flour, salt and ground nutmeg in a bowl. Make a well in the centre and pour the milk and yeast mixture into it.
- Work into a dough, then fold in the butter and egg mixture until smooth. Knead on a floured surface for 8-10 minutes.
- Shape into a ball then place in a floured bowl and cover with film. Leave to rise in a warm place for 1 hour. Turn it out onto a floured surface and knead for 2 minutes.
- Knead the raisins and sultanas into the dough along with the candied peel. Place in a springform cake tin and cover with film. Leave to prove for 2 hours in a warm place.
- Preheat the oven to 190°C (170°C fan) / 375°F / gas 5.
- Brush the top of the panettone dough with the egg white. Wrap the outside of the cake tin with aluminium foil so that it comes 10 cm above the rim of tin.
- Transfer the dough to the oven. Reduce the temperature to 180° after 15 minutes and bake for a further 30 minutes.
- Remove from the oven and leave to cool in the tin for 15 minutes. Turn out onto a wire rack to cool completely.
- Dust with the icing sugar, then slice into portions and serve from a plate.

577

SERVES 6

Mini Babas with Limoncello

Mini Babas with Amaretto

 578

Replace the Limoncello liquor with Amaretto and the lemon with an orange and prepare in the same way.

PREPARATION TIME: 35 MINUTES

COOKING TIME: 1 HOUR

INGREDIENTS

For the dough:
225 g / 8 oz of flour
125 g / 4 ½ oz of butter
20 g / ¾ oz of yeast
3 eggs
25 g / 1 oz of sugar
120 ml / 4 fl. oz / ½ cup of limoncello
3 tbsp rum
salt
For the syrup:
225 g / 8 oz / 1 cup of sugar
450 ml / 16 fl. oz / 1 pt of water
2 tbsp limoncello
1 lemon

- Prepare the dough by diluting the crumbled yeast in a little warm water and let stand for 10 minutes. Sift the flour with a pinch of salt over a bowl and make a well.

- Break the eggs into a bowl and beat them into an omelette. Place them in the well with the sugar and yeast. Mix everything with your hands and knead the dough.

- When the dough is smooth, stir in the butter cut in pieces. Place the dough in a warm place for 1 hour. The dough should have doubled in size.

- Grease small baba molds. Fill each cavity with dough half way and leave to rise for 1 hour.

- Preheat the oven to 200°C (180° fan) / 400F / gas 6.

- Cook the dough for 15 minutes. Turn out the babas and let cool.

- Prepare the syrup with lemon: cut the lemon into six slices. Put the sugar, water, limoncello, rum and lemon slices in a pan. Bring to the boil then simmer 10 minutes. Drain the lemon slices.

- Pour the hot syrup over the babas, several times so they are well soaked.

- Serve the babas with the rest of the syrup.

579

SERVES 4

Polenta and Sage Madeleines

PREPARATION TIME: 15 MINUTES

COOKING TIME: 20 MINUTES

INGREDIENTS

100 g / 4 oz ½ cup plain (all purpose) flour
80 g / 3 oz / ⅓ cup caster (superfine) sugar
2 tbsp polenta
2 eggs
1 tsp baking powder
150 ml / 5 fl. oz / ⅔ cup olive oil
1 lemon, juiced
handful sage leaves, finely sliced

- Preheat the oven to 200°C (180° fan) / 400F / gas 6.
- Oil a Madeleine mould tray and line a sage leave at the bottom of each Madeleine shape
- In a bowl, beat the eggs until frothy. Still beating, add the sugar, flour and baking powder.
- Stir in olive oil and the thinly sliced sage and carry on beating.
- Finish by adding the polenta and lemon juice.
- Once the mixture is smooth, fill the moulds with the batter and bake for 15 to 20 minutes. check for cooking with a knife point.
- Serve the Madeleines with jam or grated coconut and chocolate sauce.

Glazed Madeleines **580**
Rather than sprinkling with coconut, brush with honey for a sweeter dessert.

581

SERVES 6

Lemon Polenta Flan

PREPARATION TIME: 20 MINUTES

COOKING TIME: 30 MINUTES

INGREDIENTS

250 ml / 8 fl. oz / 1 cup of cream
500 ml / 1 pt / 2 cups of milk
150 g / 5 oz of sugar
4 eggs
125 g / 4 ½ oz of polenta
1 lemon
a Vanilla pod

- Pre-heat the oven at 180°C (160° fan) / 350F / gas 4.
- Mix the cream, milk, sugar, water, lemon juice and zest, polenta, Vanilla pod and eggs together.
- Whisk to obtain a homogeneous cream.
- Heat on medium heat, stirring constantly with a whisk.
- After about 10 minutes, the preparation will thicken.
- Turn off the heat and pour the mixture into a buttered flan tin.
- Cook for 25 minutes in the oven and cool in the refrigerator for 2 hours.
- Serve cold or slightly warmed.

Orange Polenta Flan **582**
Replace the lemon juice and zest by orange zest and orange flower water.

583
SERVES 4
Chocolate and Chestnut Tiramisu

- Whip the cream then gently fold in the chestnut puree.
- Beat the Mascarpone, 2 egg yolks and whole egg, then add the icing (confectioners') sugar.
- Combine the two mixtures.
- Soak the biscuits with the whiskey, mixed with the cocoa.
- Place the soaked crushed biscuits at the bottom of the serving dishes.
- Top with the chestnut (cob nut) mixture.
- Sprinkle with the glazed chestnuts.

PREPARATION TIME: 20 MINUTES

RESTING TIME: 1 HOUR

INGREDIENTS

250 g / 9 oz of chestnut puree
6 glazed chestnuts
150 g of whipped cream
60 ml / 2 fl. oz / ¼ cup of matured whiskey
200 g Mascarpone
35 g of icing (confectioners') sugar
1 egg
2 egg yolks
6 finger biscuits
20 g unsweetened cocoa

Panforte di Sienna

583
SERVES 8

PREPARATION TIME: 15 MINUTES

COOKING TIME: 40 MINUTES

INGREDIENTS

100 g / 4 oz candied fruit peel (oranges or lemons)
100 g / 4 oz liquid honey
100 g / 4 oz caster (superfine) sugar

50 g / 2 oz plain (all purpose) flour
75 g / 3 oz blanched hazelnuts (cob nuts)
75 g / 3 oz blanched almonds
50 g / 2 oz cocoa powder
¼ tsp of ground cinnamon
¼ tsp of allspice powder
icing (confectioners') sugar for decoration

- Preheat the oven to 160°C / 315F / gas 3.
- Finely chop the zest, and mix with the hazelnuts (cob nuts) and almonds.
- Mix everything in a bowl with the flour, cocoa, all spice and cinnamon.
- Prepare a syrup: pour the honey and sugar in a saucepan. Heat over low heat until the sugar dissolves and bring to a boil, stirring constantly, until the mix forms a ball.
- Remove from the heat and pour into the bowl, and combine everything.
- Line a cake pan with a sheet of baking paper and smooth the dough to 2 cm / 1" thick. Place in the oven and bake for 30 to 35 minutes.
- When the cake is golden brown, let it cool.
- Just before serving, dust with icing sugar passed through a fine sieve.

Tiramisu di Fragola

584
SERVES 4

PREPARATION TIME: 20 MINUTES

COOKING TIME 2 HOURS

INGREDIENTS

500 g / 1 lb 2 oz / 2 cups strawberries
250 g / 9 oz / 1 cup Mascarpone

180 g / 6 oz / 2 / 3 cup of sugar
4 eggs
½ lemon, juiced
4 tbsp strawberry syrup
2 tbsp Marsala / Amaretto
6 finger biscuits

- Wash, hull and cut the strawberries into halves, then reserve half of them for assembling. Sprinkle the remaining strawberries with lemon juice and 30 g / 1 oz of sugar. Mash the strawberries with a fork and refrigerate the mixture.
- Cut the biscuits ready to be placed in individual glasses and place them on a plate. Mix the strawberry syrup and the Marsala / Amaretto with 120 ml / 4 fl. oz / ½ cup of water. Drizzle this mixture over the biscuits in sufficient quantity to soak them well.
- Place half the biscuits in the serving glasses. Separate the yolks and whites of eggs. Beat the yolks with 120 g / 4 oz of sugar until the mixture is frothy. Add the Mascarpone and mix.
- Beat the egg whites until stiff, add the remaining sugar and gently fold the egg whites in the mascarpone mixture.
- Place a third of the strawberries over the finger biscuits, then half the strawberry mash and half the mascarpone mix.
- Repeat the process with a layer of biscuits, another third of the strawberries; the remaining strawberry mash and Mascarpone mix Finish off with the remaining strawberries and chill before serving.

585

SERVES 8

Cinnamon Prato Cookies (Cantucci)

Lemon and Hazelnut Cantucci

586

Replace the almonds with hazelnuts (cob nuts), and the cinnamon by grated lemon zest

Honey and Chocolate Cantucci

587

Replace the cinnamon with 2 tbsp of honey and 2 tbsp chocolate chips. Add some flour to the mix as it will be very sticky.

Figs and Pistachio Cantucci

588

No cinnamon in this recipes, but half the almonds are replaced by 60 g / 2 ½ oz dried figs and 2 tbsp unsalted pistachios.

PREPARATION TIME 20 MINUTES

COOKING TIME 20 MINUTES

INGREDIENTS

275 g / 10 oz / 1 ¼ cup plain (all purpose) flour
150 g / 5 oz granulated sugar
200 g / 7 oz whole almonds
3 eggs
2 tsp baking powder
5 tsp cinnamon
pinch salt
1 tsp vanilla powder

- Preheat the oven to 180°C (160° fan) / 350F / gas 4.
- In a bowl, mix with a wooden spoon the flour, sugar, baking powder, cinnamon and salt. Add the almonds.
- In a small bowl, whisk the eggs with the vanilla powder. Mix with the dry ingredients and pour over a floured surface.
- Combine for 2 minutes, regularly flouring (the dough is very sticky) until the dough is evenly mixed.
- Divide into 2 pieces and shape each piece into a sausage about 30 cm / 12" long.
- Place the rolls on a baking sheet lined with parchment paper, leaving a space of at least 10 cm between them and flatten slightly with the palm of the hand until they are 5 cm / 2" wide and 1 cm / ½" high.
- Cook for 30 minutes until the loaves are golden.
- Cool on a rack for about 30 minutes.
- Place the cooled loaves on a cutting board and using a large kitchen knife, cut diagonal slices that are returned to the oven and cooked for an extra 10 minutes until browned and crispy.

Index

Minestrone with Olives 45

Chicken and Cheese Pizzas 46

Chicken and Tomato Pizza 46

Italian Vegetable Tart 46

Mozzarella Fritters 47

Pizza Four Seasons 47

Pizza with Parma Ham 47

Ricotta Fritters 47

Creamed Yellow Pepper Soup 48

Red Pepper and Tomato Soup 48

Bruschetta 49

Bruschetta with Pesto 49

Mushroom and Basil Crostini 49

Tomato and Basil Crostini 49

Crostini with Bayonne Ham 50

Crostini with Parma Ham 50

Seafood Minestrone 50

Crostini with Artichoke and Olives 51

Crostini with Coppa 51

Mushroom and Thyme Crostini 51

Mushroom Crostini 51

Farfalle Primavera 52

Linguine Primavera 52

Minestrone and Squash 52

Minestrone with Young Spinach 52

Antipasti 53

Antipasti with Peppers 53

Grilled Parmesan Polenta 53

Grilled Polenta with Antipasti 53

Butternut Squash Gnocchi 54

Gnocchi with Spinach 54

Pumpkin and Ricotta Gnocchi 54

Pumpkin Gnocchi 54

Melon and Parma Ham 55

Melon, Parma Ham and Basil 55

Mozzarella, Ham and Chilli Salad 55

Tomato, Mozzarella and Ham Salad 55

Almond Stuffed Aubergines 56

Caponata Stuffed Aubergine 56

Italian Style Vegetables 56

Italian-Style Vegetables with Balsamic 56

Italian Brochettes with Avocado 57

Italian Brochettes with Pesto 57

Italian Summer Brochettes 57

Red Pepper Involtini 57

Yellow Pepper Involtini 57

Chilli Bread 58

Fennel Bread 58

Italian Bread 58

Onion Bread 58

Florentine Crostini 59

Florentine Sultana Crostini 59

Goat's cheese pizza 59

Tomato, Olive and Pine Nut Pizza 59

Gnocchetti alla Puttanesca 62

Gnocchetti with Red Wine 62

Tagliatelle with Green Vegetables 62

Tagliatelle with Parma Ham 62

Pasta with Artichokes and Serrano Ham 63

Red Wine Pasta 63

Mussel Pasta with Feta 64

Mussel Pasta with Lemon 64

Mussel Pasta with Red Pepper 64

Pasta with Mussels in Gorgonzola Sauce 64

Mushroom Cannelloni 65

Spinach Cannelloni with Tomato Sauce 65

Tagliatelle with Salmon and Spinach 65

Tagliatelle with Salmon and Sun Dried
 Tomatoes 65

Linguine with Salmon and Asparagus 66

Linguine with Salmon and Courgettes 66

Ravioli with Gorgonzola 66

Ravioli with Pine Nuts 66

Salmon and Pasta Salad with Asparagus 67

Smoked Salmon and Pasta Salad 67

Tagliatelle in Cream with Green Beans 67

Tagliatelle with Creamy Lemon Sauce 67

Chicken Pasta Salad with Cheese Crouton 68

Pasta Salas with Mozzarella 68

Penne Pasta Salad 68

Turkey Pasta Salad 68

Angel Hair Pasta with Parsley Sauce 69

Pasta with Peas and Parsley Sauce 69

Tortellini with Spinach and Cream 69

Tortellini with Spinach and Tomatoes 69

Vegetable and Chicken Fusilli 70

Vegetable and Turkey Fusilli 70

Spelt Pasta with Blushed Tomatoes 71

Spelt Pasta with Mediterranean 71

Spirali Pasta with Parma Ham, Parmesan and Basil
 71

Fettuccine with Pesto 72

Fettuccine with Sun-dried Tomatoes 72

Tagliatelle with Chicken and Peas 72

Tagliatelle with Mushrooms and Peas 72

Tortellini in Chilli Tomato Sauce 73

Tortellini in Creamy Tomato Sauce 73

Tortellini in Tomato Sauce 73

Tortellini with Cherry Tomatoes 73

Maltagliata with Artichokes and Confit 74

Conchiglie Stuffed with Crab 75

Tagliatelle with Tuna 75

Penne with Creamy Summer Vegetables 76

Penne with Summer Vegetables 76

Ravioli with Mushrooms 76

Chicken and Mushroom Pasta Salad 77

Chicken and Spinach Pasta Salad 77

Macaroni with Blue Cheese Sauce 77

Tagliatelle with Basil Cream Sauce 78

Linguine Bolognese 79

Linguine Bolognese with Mushrooms 79

Pasta with Mussels and Coconut 79

Pasta with Prawns and Coconut Milk 79

Spinach Tagliatelle with Cod 80

Spinach Tagliatelle with Smoked Trout 80

Three Cheese Orecchiette 80

Three Cheese Orecchiette with Tomatoes 80

Orcecchiette with Apples, Spinach and
Parma Ham 81

Orecchiette with Spinach and Bresaola 81

Penne with Green and Black Olives 81

Penne with Sun-dried Tomatoes 81

Faggottini Pasta with Basil Cream 82

Farfalle with Spicy Cherry Tomatoes 82

Tagliatelle with Leeks 82

Bollito Misto 83

Meaty Bollito Misto 83

Spaghetti with Prawns and Tomato 83

Spaghettti with Mussels and Tomato 83

Lasagna 84

Spaghetti and Anchovy Fritters 84

Spaghetti and Bacon Fritters 84

Spaghetti and Chilli Fritters 84

Spinach Lasagna 84

Conchiglie with Asparagus and Beef 85

Conchiglie with Green Beans 85

Conchiglie with Ham 85

Conchiglie with Rocket 85

Chicken Lasagna 88

Pasta with Pesto and Cod 88

Pasta with Pesto and Salmon 88

Turkey Lasagna 88

Farfalle with Aubergine 89

Farfalle with Chicken and Vegetables 89

Farfalle with Green Peppers 89

Farfalle with Prawns 89

Index